Best personal regards

— Mark

Praise for

Truth from the Trenches

and Mark Settle

"I've watched Mark Settle interact with hundreds of IT leaders. He has an instinctive ability to put his finger on the people, process, and technology issues that undermine the credibility and derail the business impact of IT teams. This book really does contain truth from the trenches of everyday experience that can benefit leaders at all levels of an IT organization."

—Adam Aarons, Chief Revenue Officer, Okta

"*Truth from the Trenches* is a no-nonsense blueprint for building and managing effective IT teams. Mark's experience as a seven-time CIO across multiple industries makes this a must-read for aspiring IT leaders."

—Chad Moss, Vice President,
Global Information Technology, IHS Markit

"Too many IT leaders sabotage their personal reputations and limit their career opportunities by making many of the missteps that are humorously illustrated in *Truth from the Trenches.* Leaders who master the fundamental management practices described in this book will earn a seat at the table where strategic business initiatives are planned and implemented."

—Lisa Jasper, Founder and Managing Partner,
Thought Ensemble

"Mark Settle has successfully incorporated emerging Silicon Valley technologies into the day-to-day operations of multiple enterprises. In doing so, he's established himself as a trusted partner to venture capitalists and start-up entrepreneurs. It's hard enough to manage a global IT team that keeps employees, customers, and partners happy. But injecting disruptive technologies into the internal operations of successful IT teams is a true art form. In this book, Mark gets to the root of how continuous innovation can become part of the intrinsic DNA of best-of-breed IT organizations."

—Arif Janmohamed, Partner, Lightspeed Venture Partners

"It takes a lot more than technical skills to become an effective IT leader. I had the good fortune of working for Mark in the past and have personally benefited from many of the less obvious, but all too true career lessons presented in *Truth from the Trenches*. I only wish that Mark had written this book sooner!"

—Ash Brooks, Global CIO, LKQ Corporation

Mark Settle understands that successful IT leaders must be able to capture the imagination of many stakeholders both within and outside their organizations. Mark helps his readers understand how to unleash the potential in their teams and in themselves—by encouraging curiosity, articulating a clear vision, skillfully exerting influence, and enabling determination by giving individuals the freedom to try, fail, and learn in the process.

—Trent Aulbaugh, Houston Office Leader,
Egon Zehnder International

TRUTH FROM THE TRENCHES

TRUTH FROM THE TRENCHES

A PRACTICAL GUIDE TO THE ART OF IT MANAGEMENT

WRITTEN BY A PRACTITIONER FOR PRACTITIONERS

MARK SETTLE

First published by Bibliomotion, Inc.
711 Third Avenue, New York, NY 10017, USA
2 Park Square, Milton Park, Abingdon, Oxon OX14 4RN, UK

Bibliomotion is an imprint of the Taylor & Francis Group, an informa business

Print ISBN 978-1-62956-193-6

CIP data has been applied for.

This book is dedicated to my three children—Patrick, Emily, and Will—may their careers be as unpredictable and rewarding as mine . . .

and to my wife, Deb, who has supported each unanticipated twist and turn of my professional journey . . .

and to the members of the teams I have been privileged to lead and learn from.

Contents

Preface

This book is a collection of observations, insights, and recommendations about how to lead and manage an IT organization. It is not intended to be a handbook or user's manual prescribing the processes required to run an IT shop. Nor is it intended to be an academic discussion of the strategic challenges confronting today's IT leaders. It is an unapologetically subjective view of the common pitfalls and opportunities faced by all IT leaders.

IT management is part science and part art form. A common framework of operational practices exists in all IT organizations. All IT shops need to respond to technical problems, update existing systems, obtain business approval for new investments, safeguard company information, and so on. Although this common framework exists, there is wide latitude in the form, substance, and prioritization of the specific work practices employed within different organizations.

Variations in work practices can be attributed to many factors, including the size of the organization, the business processes it supports, its technical sophistication, its company culture, and the prior experience of the organization's leaders. Work practices in a Fortune 500 insurance company running largely on homegrown systems will inevitably be quite different from those in a SaaS start-up company with fewer than a thousand employees.

The geographic dispersion of IT staff members can also have a big impact on internal work practices. The practices established within a highly centralized IT team based in North America tend to break down when they are extended to manage operations in different countries, time zones, and cultural settings. As businesses become more global in nature, many IT organizations learn that the processes they've developed in North America are either being openly ignored or discreetly subverted in their overseas offices.

Consequently, there is no one right way to manage an IT organization. But there are many chronic pitfalls. One of the primary purposes of this book is to identify the pitfalls that can so easily undermine the success of aspiring IT leaders.

IT management is more of a craft that needs to be honed through on-the-job experience than a profession that can be learned in a classroom. Many professions such as law and accounting have rigorous certification processes to ensure the consistency and integrity of the work practices employed by their practitioners. There is no comparable certification process for IT management. Even widely accepted management frameworks for software development (e.g., the Carnegie Mellon Capability Maturity Model) or IT operations (e.g., the Information Technology Infrastructure Library [ITIL]) are nothing more than a collection of guidelines. They are not codified bodies of knowledge that must be followed in detail to obtain external certification. ITIL consultants will frequently tell you that the ITIL framework is not a prescriptive "cookbook" of best practices. Rather it should be treated as a book *about* cooking. Each IT shop needs to develop its own unique set of operational practices.

From my admittedly biased perspective, I believe that managing IT is more complex than managing many of the other corporate functions in a global enterprise. Finance teams follow a work schedule that is largely prescribed by the monthly accounting close, the quarterly close, the quarterly earnings call with investment analysts, board meetings, and external presentations at investor conferences. They are required to adhere to a variety of fiduciary standards and regulatory requirements. The integrity of their internal processes is reviewed continuously by internal and external auditors and reported to the Audit Committee at every Board of Directors meeting. Similarly, Human Resources (HR) administers a prescribed set of programs, including employee performance reviews, merit and bonus awards, benefits enrollment, succession planning, applicant tracking, etc. Although HR work processes are not audited explicitly, HR also operates within a stringent regulatory environment and needs to avoid creating liabilities for the company by failing to comply with such regulations.

Success in functions such as Finance and HR can be measured in terms of completing prescribed activities on schedule and in strict compliance with all relevant external standards and regulatory rules. IT success is more difficult to measure because there are far fewer prescribed activities, and success is largely based on the perceptions of business colleagues who consume IT services. For example, the finance team can produce a flawless 10-Q report on a company's quarterly performance that is judged to be successful by the SEC, the board, and the company's auditors. In contrast, IT can expand network capacity or upgrade the CRM system, but the success of such initiatives will ultimately be judged by business colleagues who employ these capabilities to perform their jobs.

I believe this contrast exists with other functional groups as well. Manufacturing and supply chain operations have well-established metrics regarding throughput, unit costs, and inventory velocity that must be met to achieve predetermined returns on investment or working capital. Sales and marketing teams also have objective performance metrics regarding lead generation, quota coverage, deal closure rates, and subscription renewal rates. If properly managed, none of these functions relies on internal perceptions to judge its success. All have established success metrics that are accepted and respected by other functional groups. In contrast, IT typically establishes a set of technical metrics to manage internal operations, but these metrics are unknown or poorly understood by business leaders. There are many, many cases where IT credibility is low even while the technical metrics being used to track internal operations are at or above targeted levels.

Experiential learning becomes the primary educational mechanism in a profession that lacks formal certifications and relies on its customers to define success. Although I hesitate to claim that effective IT management practices can only be developed through trial and error, I am convinced that they cannot be taught in the classroom. Much like medieval artisans, accomplished IT leaders have typically passed through apprentice and journeyman stages in their careers before achieving the skills and status of master craftsmen.

They Don't Teach Real-World IT in School

If you believe that colleges prepare students for careers in the IT industry, you should spend a day manning a recruiting booth at a campus job fair for summer interns. College students generally understand the processes involved in developing applications or building websites. They can readily relate to roles they might play in coding and testing application software. However, when you start to describe other projects they might encounter during a summer internship experience, their eyes glaze over and they rapidly lose interest because they have no earthly idea what you are talking about. Typical work assignments for summer students might include resolving CMDB discrepancies created by different infrastructure discovery tools; optimizing extract/transform/load procedures for nightly updates to the data warehouse; documenting user requirements and building scripts to test such requirements; tuning intrusion detection tools to reduce the occurrence of false positive events; testing upgrades to hardware or software systems before they are put in production; and evaluating competitive product offerings from two or more vendors. These are basic bread-and-butter activities within any IT shop, but they are totally beyond the comprehension of undergrads at most, if not all, major universities.

IT management is a full-contact sport, not to be pursued by the faint of heart. IT organizations are essentially confederations of tribal teams that individually possess unique technical skills or knowledge. For their collective survival, these technical tribes band together and establish internal work practices to address the needs of their external business clients. A high degree of daily interaction is required within the confederation itself, simply to deliver on IT's commitments to its clients. A second and equally daunting set of relationships needs to be cultivated with the clients who are ultimately footing the bill for IT's expenses. All IT leaders must establish effective interpersonal relationships both within and outside the IT organization to be truly successful. Unfortunately, many IT leaders lack the disposition and social skills required to manage such relationships productively.

On a good day, IT management resembles a championship NFL football team, rotating individuals with highly specialized skills onto the field of play and employing a wide variety of formations and strategies to succeed. Tactics may be altered at the line of scrimmage on any given play, but consistently successful teams establish strategic game plans that leverage their intrinsic strengths and exploit their opponent's weaknesses. On a bad day, IT management resembles a mediocre NFL team, lining up incorrectly at the line of scrimmage, losing ground through self-inflicted penalties, and failing to perform due to talent deficiencies or communication breakdowns. Repeated failures to score points undermine the morale and focus of the team. By the end of the game, the offense looks defeated before the players even line up.

There are many existing books on IT management. I was motivated to write this book for three reasons. First, many of the fundamental issues that undermine the effectiveness of IT organizations are chronic in nature and still exist today. Most IT shops carry a tremendous technical debt, maintaining legacy systems based upon antiquated technologies simply because there's no business justification for the investments required to upgrade such systems. Technical debt can extend deeply into the ranks of the technical staff as well. The majority of IT staff members may have little familiarity with emerging technologies or modern operational practices. Technical leaders continue to be promoted into people management roles for which they have very little aptitude or experience. Many such leaders spend more time doing the jobs of their subordinates, further undermining morale and initiative, when they should be focused on expanding the skills and responsibilities of their team members. Finally, IT organizations have an instinctive tendency to spend more time talking to themselves than communicating with their external customers. Failure to communicate with the stakeholders that are ultimately footing the bill for IT's services is a prescription for irrelevance. Failure to educate business leaders about how to leverage new, emerging technologies is equally self-limiting.

These three cardinal sins—talent debt, ineffective people management, and failure to establish productive working relationships with business partners—are responsible for the shortcomings of most IT organizations. Transformational IT initiatives will achieve only limited results or fail altogether unless these foundational issues are rectified through a dedicated focus on upgrading talent, managing staff productivity, and cultivating business relationships. Suggestions regarding all three of these foundational issues are presented in this book.

My second motivation for writing this book is to address the shocking failure of IT leaders to benefit from the learnings of their predecessors. Perhaps because IT management is more craft than science and effective management skills can only be honed through on-the-job training, this failure to convey best practices is predictable. Nevertheless, after three decades of industry experience, I remain shocked at the extent to which best practices need to be relearned on a trial-and-error basis by successive generations of IT leaders. In all too many IT organizations, managers are unwittingly mimicking the actors in the movie *Groundhog Day*, endlessly repeating the same meaningless tasks, committing the same mistakes, and solving the same problems as their predecessors!

Personal Groundhog Day Experience

In a past life, I led an IT organization that experienced the wholesale failure of its primary data center during prime shift in North America. It turned out that one of the network engineers had decided to upgrade the software on the primary network switch within the data center during a normal workday. He committed an error during the upgrade that tripped the switch, suspending all network communications in and out of the data center. When I asked if we had procedures that restricted network upgrades to nonbusiness hours I was told, "Oh yes, that is our procedure—we just didn't follow it." Further investigation revealed that the engineer's son had a birthday party the following weekend. He attempted the upgrade during the work week so he could devote his full attention to his son's party over the weekend. This stuff really happens... you can't make it up!

Major battles over business initiatives, technology road maps, and IT investment strategies are rarely won with pretty viewgraph presentations in large conference rooms. They are won through a series of small unit actions that precede such meetings. They are won by mobilizing the necessary talent, selecting the appropriate vendors, and igniting the imagination of business unit leaders. They are won through a series of guerilla tactics that align the enthusiasm and dedication of key IT staff members, business colleagues, and vendor specialists around a common goal. The success of any IT strategy or initiative depends upon the enlightened intervention of IT managers at critical junctures to solicit stakeholder feedback, make tactical decisions, preserve team alignment, and maintain focus on near-term objectives. This doesn't happen automatically, it doesn't happen easily, and it doesn't happen without a special combination of technical, business, and interpersonal skills. This book will school its readers in some of the critical small unit tactics that successful IT leaders employ to overcome the centrifugal forces that threaten the performance and credibility of their organizations.

Finally, in the interest of full disclosure, I must admit that my third motivation for writing this book is personal catharsis. I have personally committed many of the mistakes discussed in the ensuing chapters. I've visited other organizations suffering from similar flaws. Whether the management pitfalls discussed in this book were of my own making or created by others, they ultimately resulted in staff frustration, failure to deliver on business commitments, and lost opportunities. After years of obtaining hard-won insights into the mistakes that commonly undermine the performance of an IT organization, I've used this book as an emotional safety valve to vent my personal convictions regarding effective IT management practices.

Some may criticize this book as being overly focused on the inner workings of IT organizations when the real challenge facing IT leaders today is their ability to establish transformational business strategies that will spur top-line growth or enhance the profitability of their companies. These are laudable goals but they can't be addressed if the IT organization fails to perform its routine duties in a reliable fashion or if the members of the organization fail to support the strategic agendas of their leaders. This book is all about developing the internal competence and external credibility required to earn a place at the executive table, where transformational business strategies are debated and launched.

This book is written by a veteran IT practitioner for IT practitioners. It is not based upon academic theories, industry surveys, or consulting engagements. It is a worm's-eye view written from the trenches of practical experience. Over the past three decades, I have been fortunate to work in a wide variety of industries and Fortune 500 companies. I survived the Y2K hysteria; the implementation of monolithic ERP, CRM, and SCM systems; the bursting of the Internet 1.0 bubble; the advent of eCommerce, SaaS, data center virtualization, and cloud computing; and the current obsession with mobility, collaboration, Big Data, and information security. I've worked for companies of widely varying sizes with extensive international operations. I've worked for companies that consume IT products and services and for vendors that supply such products and services. My career has easily exceeded the ten thousand–hour threshold required to achieve mastery in any given profession, as popularized in Malcolm Gladwell's book *Outliers*. My personal on-the-job experiences and the opportunities I've had to observe other IT organizations form the basis for the insights and opinions presented in this book.

Over the course of my career I have slowly come to realize that the issues undermining the success of the organizations I have led were largely the same. Individual companies may have operated in different industries with different business models. Executive management teams may have had different personalities and proclivities. The financial circumstances that impacted the size and scope of IT investments may have varied as well. But almost invariably the external forces and self-inflicted wounds that limited IT's effectiveness remained largely the same. This book provides practical advice about managing those forces and cauterizing the most common wounds.

Although this book is written from a CIO's perspective, the pitfalls and best practices presented here can be leveraged by anyone in an IT leadership role who manages budgets, talent, customers, operations, vendors, or innovation. This book will be a runaway success if its readers can find one idea or learning they can employ to improve the effectiveness of their team or the credibility of their organization. I've invested a considerable amount of personal sweat equity in building processes, relationships, and initiatives that yielded minimal or nonexistent benefits. Hopefully, the readers of this book will achieve a higher return on their professional sweat equity by following some of the suggestions and avoiding some of the pitfalls discussed in the following chapters.

To those readers who have worked with me in the past, I ask your indulgence. You have already been subjected to my personal convictions regarding IT management. You will be painfully familiar with the recommendations presented in this book!

Mark Settle
San Francisco
October 2016

Prologue

Leadership Versus Management

Leadership and management are all too often discussed as two mutually exclusive sets of capabilities and accomplishments. Leadership is invariably described as the superior skill set exercised by an exclusive group of exceptional individuals, while management skills are considered to be more mundane and commonplace. Leadership skills are held in such high esteem that they are sometimes regarded as inborn or genetic while management skills can be learned through training and experience.

I don't personally subscribe to this polar distinction between leadership and management. Leaders don't stop exercising their management skills when they cross some magical threshold in their careers. The management actions they take and the management decisions they make are the primary means of validating their leadership capabilities. While not all managers will become leaders, leaders will continue to manage but they will do so in different ways. The principal distinction between a leader and a manager is the manner in which a leader goes about fulfilling his formal responsibilities and the ways in which he employs his discretionary time and effort.

Capable leaders surround themselves with talented individuals and delegate effectively. They establish processes that provide checks and balances on the parochial interests of individual work teams and facilitate organizational alignment around common goals and priorities. Capable leaders hold themselves and their teams accountable. They don't sidestep discussions of performance issues or failures. They communicate continuously and credibly with major and minor stakeholders. And they inspire their teams to deliver results that exceed customer expectations in terms of timing, cost, quality, or quantity. Leaders avoid the temptation to micromanage their teams' activities and routinely convert such impulses into career development opportunities for individual team members.

Capable managers deliver expected results on time and on budget. They complete routine assignments without being monitored or prodded. They continually strive to find ways of improving the efficiency of their teams, commonly through the use of operational metrics. They are typically respected and liked by their team members. Capable managers may rarely exceed expectations but they minimize the risk of technical or financial failure and enhance stakeholder perceptions regarding the competence and reliability of the IT organization. Every IT organization needs capable managers—lots of them—to be successful.

Leaders employ their discretionary time and effort in creative ways that improve the productivity and business impact of their teams. Some may cultivate relationships with external stakeholders that have been overlooked or ignored in the past. Others may evaluate the effectiveness of internal work practices by consulting peers in other companies or employing the services of management consultants. Some may investigate the capabilities of new tools or set aside time for advanced training in the use of existing tools and services. Still others may play a personal role in coaching team members who have exhibited leadership capabilities in their current assignments.

Discretionary pursuits typically expand the agility and work capacity of a leader's organization, enabling it to assume broader responsibilities in the future. Team members commonly find themselves doing things that were inconceivable only twelve months earlier because the leader has expanded the organization's capabilities in ways that were unknown or thought to be impossible.

We have to disabuse ourselves of the notion that management is somehow dirty work that is routinely minimized or avoided by leaders. From a leader's perspective, leadership and management are two sides of the same coin. IT leaders are not prophets or oracles who inspire their followers to feats of glory with grand visions and rhetorical eloquence. IT leaders can't achieve their strategic or transformational objectives without taking myriad management actions and decisions that turn their visions into reality. IT teams have learned through years of experience to pay attention to what their leaders actually do and not necessarily to what they say. The management actions that leaders take serve as proof points of their leadership capabilities in the eyes of their teams.

Management reputations are earned, typically over a period of years. Individuals who consistently deliver expected results, operate within budgetary guidelines, keep their teams motivated and productive, collaborate constructively with their peers, and communicate effectively with external stakeholders are inevitably regarded as good managers. Management competencies lend themselves to self-assessment. Individual managers can readily compare their accomplishments to those of their peers and draw reasonably accurate conclusions regarding their personal management capabilities.

Leadership reputations, on the other hand, are conferred. They are conferred by the members of the leader's team. They are conferred by the leader's peers and by her superiors. Individuals may undertake initiatives and fulfill their assigned responsibilities in ways that they perceive to be creative, but until their initiative and creativity are appreciated by others, they are not considered to be true leaders.

Good managers who aspire to become leaders are embarking on a difficult and risky journey, precisely because there is no set formula of skills and behaviors that define impactful leadership and because leadership is ultimately established through the recognition of others. Anyone in an IT management position or senior technical role will have an opportunity to develop and display her leadership capabilities. Those who elect to play it safe and merely fulfill their assigned responsibilities will accomplish little more than enhancing their current management reputations.

Because of the intimate association between leadership and management practices, the terms leadership and management are used somewhat interchangeably in this book. But make no mistake: the management recommendations presented in this book are designed to advance the leadership ambitions of its readers. The advice presented in this book should enable the reader to develop more creative ways of meeting current commitments and suggest a variety of extracurricular pursuits that will enhance the capabilities of her team. That is the true path to IT leadership.

Chapter 1

Follow the Money

It's a sad commentary that a book on IT management starts with a discussion of financial management practices and relegates the topic of technology innovation to one of its closing chapters. Perhaps this initial emphasis on money management is inevitable, since so many business conversations regarding IT start and end with a discussion of IT costs.

IT organizations spend a lot of money. IT spending as a percent of a company's revenues is a largely meaningless metric because there are so many factors that impact the nature of IT expenses and the accounting practices used to track them. IT spending commonly represents 5 to 10 percent of the total operating expenses within a large enterprise. IT staffing levels may vary from 3 to 10 percent of the total employee population. Obviously, these percentages are approximate and will vary considerably among different companies and industries. But by any measure, the level of IT spending is significant in any large commercial enterprise.

Where does all that money go? While IT leaders believe they are barely getting by on their existing budgets and struggling to maintain aging systems that desperately need to be replaced, their business counterparts are continually asking, "Why does IT cost so much and what do all those people do?" Unfortunately, some IT leaders react to such statements as personal accusations of financial incompetence, when in fact they are statements of ignorance. Business leaders are chronically frustrated by IT spending levels because they truly have no comprehension of the IT infrastructure that supports a company's daily business operations. Each functional group or business unit has a narrow understanding of the systems and tools they employ to perform their jobs. But they have no conception of the full portfolio of business applications employed throughout the corporation or the underlying technologies required for the use of such applications.

Paradoxically, naïve business perceptions regarding IT costs are a direct result of the success of the IT organization. The IT capabilities within most large enterprises are largely taken for granted. Email is readily accessible on PCs and mobile devices; work files are available on shared drives or SharePoint; business-critical applications and databases are continually enhanced and updated; Skype can be used to collaborate with colleagues via text or video; and all these capabilities are globally accessible on a 24×7 basis. Employees outside IT—including business executives—have very little appreciation of the engineering and support activities required to keep essential IT services working every day.

Taking IT for Granted

New employee onboarding is a complicated and contentious process in many companies. New employees can get off to a rocky start in their relationship with IT if they don't receive the equipment, licenses, access rights, and training they need in a timely fashion. (To most new employees, "timely" means their first day on the job!) Many IT shops take great pride in the efficiency of their employee onboarding practices, but I've always found it useful to contact one or two new hires on a periodic basis to obtain firsthand feedback about their onboarding experiences. In one instance I contacted a recently hired sales executive to inquire about his interactions with IT during his first few weeks on the job. He was shocked to find a fully functional PC waiting for him on his first day at work. He told me that it typically took new employees one to two weeks to receive PCs at his old company. Then he complimented me on our company-wide wifi network. He told me that wifi capabilities at his old company were limited to a select number of major offices. He was absolutely floored by the ability to seamlessly connect to the company network at the offices he had visited thus far—irrespective of their size or location. I hadn't received compliments regarding employee onboarding or wifi connectivity in a long time, and immediately realized that our existing employees were no longer impressed by such services because they simply took them for granted. It was actually refreshing to hear someone express appreciation for such services for a change!

Although information technology is frequently discussed as a strategic corporate asset or a source of competitive advantage, IT spending occupies one of the least strategic positions on a company's profit and loss (P&L) statement. Most, if not all, IT spending is reported externally as a general and administrative (G&A) expense. Unlike the cost of goods sold, selling expenses, or R&D investments, G&A spending is considered to be the cost of unavoidable overhead activities required to run a corporation. G&A spending is commonly treated as a tax on the profit-generating activities within a company and rarely, if ever, perceived to be strategic in nature. External financial analysts continually scrutinize G&A expenses and expect them to decrease as a percentage of total company revenues as a company grows. These external expectations provide business executives with further incentives to curb IT spending.

How to Talk to Business Leaders About IT Spending

IT leaders commonly approach spending discussions with business executives as instructional opportunities. They fervently, if naïvely, believe that business leaders would appreciate the cost effectiveness of the company's current IT capabilities if they only had a deeper understanding of the technical and operational issues involved in delivering specific IT services. Consequently, they adopt the role of instructors trying to teach business leaders about the technical challenges and cost implications of integrating, operating, and maintaining complex IT systems. A tutorial approach to rationalizing IT expenses rarely succeeds, however, because most business executives don't have the time, interest, or background needed to absorb the technology lessons being presented. Business executives view such discussions as opportunities to assess the financial knowledge and credibility of IT leaders, not as college colloquia where they can learn more about the architecture of IT systems.

IT leaders should approach spending discussions with their business counterparts as financial exams and prepare for them accordingly. If the activity under discussion involves a variety of labor resources (e.g., internal staff, outsourced staff, consultants, or contractors), the IT leader should know the unit cost and total cost of each resource pool. If new or existing vendor capabilities are under discussion, the IT leader should be conversant about the pricing of vendor products and propose creative ways of procuring incremental capabilities. If the activity under discussion is a common capability that exists in most companies—such as service desk operations—it's always helpful to reference industry-average or best-in-class cost comparisons established through external benchmarking studies. Business executives participating in IT spending discussions will rarely remember the particulars of what was actually discussed but they will form definite opinions about the financial competence of their IT counterparts. If IT leaders are perceived to be knowledgeable financial managers, most business executives will devote much less time to second-guessing IT expenditures because they realize that they can add very little value to such discussions.

A second trap to avoid in IT spending discussions is a focus on cost categories. Standard cost categories include such things as labor, consulting, telecom, software, travel, and training expenses. If IT leaders fail to provide an alternative lens for viewing IT expenses, their business counterparts will soon be asking random questions about spending trends and variances at the category level. For example, they may ask why IT travel costs have gone up 20 percent relative to the previous quarter (answer: overseas travel was required to close the Ireland data center); or why consulting expenses have increased over the past two quarters (answer: consultants are being used to reengineer order management processes as part of the recently approved Quote-to-Cash project); or why telecom expenses are so much larger year over year (answer: we have more employees following last year's acquisition). There are usually very good answers to random cost variance questions, but the answers may not always be obvious and may require additional analysis. Public displays of ignorance during cost variance discussions do not inspire business confidence or credibility. They obviously have exactly the opposite effect.

The best possible lens that can be applied to IT spending is one that reflects the business or functional structure of the company. To the extent that large chunks of IT spending can be associated with key value-generating activities—such as sales and marketing, R&D, or manufacturing—the easier it will be to discuss IT expenses with business leaders. Very few business executives think that their companies will be more successful if software or telecom expenses increase on a quarterly basis. But those same executives would commend IT for increasing expenditures on new capabilities that will improve the effectiveness of the company's sales and marketing teams.

It's naïve to think that IT leaders can avoid spending discussions at a cost category level altogether. But they should, to the best of their ability, recast these conversations in terms of the company's key business operations. There have been countless books, workshops, and conferences devoted to the importance of "aligning IT with the business." In the minds of most business executives, IT alignment has little to do with ethereal debates about leveraging technology to retain customers, expand market share, or improve profit margins. In their minds, IT alignment is all about how much IT spending is being devoted to their functional group or business unit. If they're satisfied that their team is receiving its fair share (or more) of the IT pie, they will be largely satisfied that IT is aligned with the business (i.e., *their* business!).

The IT Spending Pendulum

A perpetual motion machine is a purely hypothetical notion that provides an apt analogy for IT spending discussions. In theory, perpetual motion machines perform work indefinitely without an obvious energy source. In practice, IT spending discussions can go on indefinitely, sometimes for no apparent reason. Spending discussions in large enterprises continually oscillate between the cost of new initiatives and the cost of current operations. IT managers are fated to spend significant portions of their careers soliciting funds for new initiatives while continually reducing the residual costs of past investments.

The IT spending pendulum moves back and forth with maddening regularity—sometimes several times within a single day or week! IT leaders engage in a never-ending stream of discussions, emails, and meetings to develop detailed plans for new initiatives. Such plans evolve through iterative interactions with IT staff members, business partners, and vendors that may persist for months or quarters before an initiative is ultimately approved or rejected. At the same time, IT leaders are continually confronted by the need to reduce different aspects of IT spending. Project overruns in the application group may necessitate offsetting reductions in infrastructure spending. The CEO may be concerned about the rise in travel expenses and initiate a company-wide campaign to curtail travel. The CFO may be taxing all functional groups to divert funds for the expansion of the company's sales force. Cost reduction conversations don't occur on a one-time basis when the annual budget is being constructed. They are an intrinsic, inescapable component of the ongoing management dialog within every IT organization.

Few individuals who aspire to IT leadership roles are fully prepared for the emotional vertigo that's induced by the constant oscillation between planning new initiatives and dismantling past ones. A true leader needs a deep inner reserve of emotional fortitude to maintain public optimism about the eventual success of new funding proposals while dissipating the pervasive pessimism created by ongoing cost reductions.

As indicated above, spending cuts may be required at any time and for a wide variety of reasons. They may be self-induced by a need to offset cost overruns elsewhere in the IT organization. Alternatively, the company may simply have had a "bad quarter" and the CFO may ask all groups to curtail unnecessary spending during the next three months. Astute IT leaders maintain private lists of potential expense reductions to respond to such demands on short notice. These lists are not static. They are continually groomed and updated as new information comes to light regarding the nature, size, and timing of different cost-cutting opportunities.

It's difficult to explore cost-reduction opportunities within an IT organization without triggering anxieties among the staff, either intentionally or inadvertently. Questions or information requests that may appear casual or innocuous to an IT manager can provoke deep-seated fears of technology changes, organizational restructuring, or even layoffs among staff members. IT leaders who have the foresight to proactively investigate cost-cutting opportunities within their organizations need to openly communicate the purpose, scope, and timing of such investigations. Many leaders withhold such information from their teams to avoid triggering anxieties. Such strategies rarely succeed and merely fuel the local rumor mill within the leader's organization.

True Leaders Should Always Be Prepared to Cut Costs

IT organizations always have more ideas about how to spend money than save money. That's a fundamental law of nature within IT! Leaders who continually investigate savings opportunities within their organizations are not only prepared to respond to cost-reduction demands, they can also apply such savings to internal needs or opportunities without having to beg for additional funding from their business partners. Experience has shown that redeploying funds in this manner is best performed during the first two to three quarters of a fiscal year. Annual budgeting processes typically establish spending projections for the next fiscal year on the basis of actual plus planned expenditures during the last three to four months of the current fiscal year. If self-inflicted savings realized during the last third of a fiscal year are not immediately reinvested, they will inadvertently lower the spending baseline for the following year. IT leaders need to manage the timing of self-initiated expense reductions carefully to ensure that their savings aren't redeployed elsewhere within the corporation.

Negotiating spending reductions with business executives requires the skills of a seasoned poker player. It's best not to show all your cards too early in the process. A delicate balance needs to be struck between being overly accommodating and overly defensive. IT leaders can boost their business credibility by responding to reduction demands promptly with a carefully crafted set of initiatives. The consequences of each initiative—both short term and long term—should be expressed in business terms whenever possible. IT leaders should educate their business colleagues about the pain that will accompany the prospective cuts, but they should also exhibit a clear willingness to absorb such pain for the greater good of the corporation. If IT leaders respond to cost-cutting demands too quickly or if the pain associated with individual reductions is expressed solely in IT terms, the leader may be asked to dig deeper and find additional savings. On the other hand, leaders who resist reduction demands and persistently defend current spending levels rarely succeed in avoiding budget cuts and can lose their business credibility in the process. In summary, IT leaders faced with cost-reduction demands need to respond in a proactive but calculated fashion. They need to present cost-cutting plans that clearly delineate the business consequences of individual expense reductions. Furthermore, they shouldn't be the first of their peers to respond to such demands, but neither should they be the last.

Ancient Days of IT Budgeting

In the early stages of my career I was required to construct an annual spending plan for my team as part of my company's annual budgeting process. In addition, I was explicitly required to identify expenses that could be reduced or eliminated if my funding request was decreased by 5, 10, or 15 percent. I was also required to identify incremental purchases or activities that would be pursued if my budget request was increased by 5, 10, or 15 percent. This procedure gave senior management the ability to redeploy budget funds from groups with the least painful reduction opportunities to groups with the most beneficial investment opportunities. It was widely used within large enterprises to exchange downside pain for upside gains across disparate technical teams. Over the years, this procedure has become increasingly one sided. CEOs and CFOs routinely challenge the annual spending plans submitted by their IT groups and inquire about the impact of potential reductions. However, they rarely, if ever, inquire about the benefits that might be realized by increasing IT's annual funding request.

As indicated above, one of the smartest strategies for discussing IT costs is to fence off chunks of IT spending that can be associated with specific business operations, preferably those operations that are universally regarded as revenue generating. For example, B2C businesses typically spend a lot of money on consumer marketing and make extensive use of web-based systems to attract new customers and expand sales to existing ones. IT spending on marketing and web operations within these types of companies is sacrosanct and will rarely be challenged by business executives. A similar example exists when IT supports software teams developing new commercial products. IT spending on development tools and environments will rarely be questioned in companies that rely on software development for revenue growth.

There's no standard business classification framework for IT expenses. Every IT leader needs to establish a system for classifying IT costs that will intuitively resonate with the perceptions of their business peers. It's not necessary to associate all IT expenditures with specific business functions or organizations, but where such associations can be easily constructed they should be established and freely shared with business partners. Financial precision is not necessarily required for such discussions. Reasonable estimates of spending levels or spending ranges will suffice.

The Washington Monument Strategy for Fencing Expenses

I spent the early stages of my career working for the federal government. During one of my first encounters with the federal budgeting cycle, I was asked to prepare a plan for absorbing a 10 percent cut to my organization's current budget. My boss asked me to build my reduction plan around the closure of a data center that just happened to be in the home district of a U.S. representative who was one of our biggest supporters on Capitol Hill. I was aghast, and told him that we would never be permitted to close that center. He grinned at me and said, "Of course not, that's the Washington Monument strategy."

When I inquired what the term "Washington Monument strategy" meant, he told me that whenever the Office of Management & Budget (OMB) asked the National Park Service (NPS) to cut its budget, the NPS would agree and announce that access to the Washington Monument was being terminated as a cost-savings measure. The Washington Monument is one of the principal destinations of schoolchildren who flock to the U.S. capital every year. If the nation's schoolchildren were frustrated by lack of access to the monument their voting parents would be upset. And if the parents were upset their congressional representatives would become angry. OMB had no interest in staging a pitched battle with the U.S. Congress over access to the Washington Monument. Consequently, OMB would ultimately back down from its demands for NPS budget cuts, giving rise to the term Washington Monument strategy.

When faced with expense-reduction demands, practitioners of the Washington Monument strategy put the products and services that are most highly valued by their customers at the top of the cut list. By building our budget-reduction plan around the closure of a data center in the home district of this particular representative, we were assured that the reduction would never actually occur (and it didn't!).

Getting Everyone in the Game

I once worked for a company that conducted career development reviews for all employees on an annual basis. To prepare for these discussions, the employees were asked to document their short-term career goals over the next one to two years and their longer-term goals over the next three to five years. More than half the members of the IT organization routinely indicated that they wanted to become VPs or CIOs within the next three to five years.

This particular company employed a large number of cost centers to track expenditures at a fairly granular level. Although this accounting framework created a lot of administrative busywork, it gave staff members an opportunity to develop some elementary skills in budgeting and expense management. Surprisingly (or predictably?) most staff members had no interest in becoming cost center managers. Ironically, the same individuals who expressed keen interest in becoming IT executives actively avoided any type of financial management responsibility.

IT managers and technical leaders frequently have very limited understanding of basic financial mechanics. They don't always understand the differences between capital and operating expenditures. They don't necessarily understand how capitalized expenditures are reflected in future depreciation charges. They don't appreciate the importance of correctly associating invoices with approved purchase orders or ensuring that time cards are filled out appropriately. This is pretty basic stuff but there's a pervasive sense in most IT organizations that managing and tracking costs is someone else's responsibility.

One of the critical financial challenges every IT leader faces is ensuring that all managers and technical leaders understand the financial commitments IT has made to its business partners. Furthermore, they need to fully understand the rules, procedures, and initiatives that have been established to deliver on those commitments. No one person can be responsible for achieving financial targets within a large, complex IT organization. Financial discipline is the responsibility of the entire management team.

Quarterly business reviews (QBRs) focused exclusively on IT finances can be an effective means of ensuring that all department managers and technical leaders understand the current financial status of the overall IT organization. These meetings don't necessarily need to be long or formal or require a lot of preparation. They should serve as level setting discussions that ensure the consistent dissemination of up-to-date financial information. (In many companies, managers and technical leaders participate in bonus programs that are based in whole or in part on the financial performance of the IT organization. Consistent communication of financial information under these circumstances can pay big dividends in fostering the teamwork needed to achieve budget targets.)

Financial management responsibilities need to be shared and delegated in ways that don't trigger mass financial hysteria within the organization. An unrelenting focus on cost control can actually be counterproductive. It can trigger obsessive-compulsive behaviors that distract staff members from their responsibilities and undermine their productivity.

Obsessive-compulsive disorders (OCD) are defined as states of recurring anxiety characterized by uncontrollable thoughts and repetitive behaviors that individuals feel compelled to perform. IT organizations suffering from persistent financial anxiety have uncontrollable thoughts about future pay cuts and layoffs. Consequently, they feel compelled to examine every incremental expense and debate its necessity regardless of its size or criticality. IT shops exhibiting financial OCD behaviors routinely reject standard travel requests, cancel needed training, badger vendors for inconsequential discounts, and suspend orders for routine supplies. Managers need to be on the lookout for such behaviors and curb them immediately, before they sabotage the performance of the entire organization.

It's quite common for IT managers to become obsessively concerned with managing negative cost variances (i.e., overspending relative to budget) while devoting little time or attention to cultivating positive cost variances. Exhaustive analysis goes into determining the causes of negative variances and developing action plans that limit or reverse their growth. In contrast, most managers spend very little time trying to achieve positive cost variances on business-as-usual activities. For example, if contractors were employed to perform a specific task over an eight-week period and 70 percent of the work was completed after the first month on the job, few managers would attempt to accelerate the remaining work and terminate the contractors after six weeks. Savings (positive variances) can also be routinely achieved by reassigning unused software licenses instead of buying new ones, eliminating maintenance contracts on equipment that is not business critical, or establishing rules for recovering underutilized server or storage capacity. There are multiple ways of reducing costs within an IT organization, but if such costs are within budget they are routinely incurred without a second thought.

Enlightened IT leaders find ways of incorporating prospective savings opportunities in the financial scorecards they share with their management teams. Leaders are generally quite adept at identifying the financial risks associated with specific projects or activities or procurements. They are less practiced at identifying savings opportunities embedded in business-as-usual activities. Upside financial opportunities are realized when consultants or contractors are employed for shorter periods of time than originally planned; when the purchase of vendor products or services can be delayed; when the start dates for new hires are pushed beyond the end of the quarter; when vendor contracts are recompeted instead of being automatically renegotiated; and so on. Project savings can be achieved by levying a 10 percent tax on all new projects to create a collective contingency fund. Most self-respecting project managers will do their best to deliver targeted results within their remaining budgets without appealing for contingency funding. Unused contingency money represents another cost-savings opportunity.

IT leaders need to adopt a much more balanced approach to managing positive and negative budget variances, and they need to incent their teams accordingly. Managers are routinely penalized for cost overruns but rarely rewarded on a commensurate basis for pursuing savings opportunities. Management reward systems need to be reengineered to rectify this imbalance.

The Benefits of Fixed-Price Contract Management Experience

Fixed-price contracts are widely used in both the public and private sectors to manage financial risk. In a fixed-price contract, the contractor estimates the expenditures required to satisfy a customer's requirements and then adds overhead expenses and a measure of profit to his cost proposal. If anything unexpected happens over the life of the contract, the contractor either has to negotiate a formal change order with the customer to obtain additional funds or absorb the financial consequences of the unanticipated change.

Many IT shops employ fixed-price contracts on major projects as a means of shifting the risk of unanticipated cost overruns onto the contractor instead of themselves. Inevitably, some aspects of the plans established at the outset of a project turn out to be easier to accomplish while others prove to be much harder. To maximize profit, the contractor needs to find ways of completing tasks ahead of schedule, discharging expensive individuals with highly specialized skills as early as possible, deferring hardware and software purchases as long as possible, and taking immediate corrective action when any individual task jeopardizes the on-time completion of the project.

Fixed-price contract managers develop a maniacal focus on schedule and scope management. They are constantly seeking ways of achieving positive cost variances (i.e., savings) that provide a financial hedge against negative variances (i.e., overruns) that will inevitably occur. This discipline rarely exists within an IT organization because the systems needed to track schedules and costs at a task level simply don't exist. And besides, as long as actual costs don't exceed budgeted costs, nobody really cares! For example: When was the last time you heard a member of your management team report the early completion of a task on a project's critical path, or take credit for reducing the time-to-completion of a specific activity? Sad to say, most IT organizations manage their costs in the same way that government bureaucrats manage their budgets. In both cases, their goal is to spend the entire budget allotted to an individual task or activity.

CFOs are always seeking ways of improving their company's operating leverage to ensure that revenues and profits are able to grow faster than operating expenses in the future. Most CFOs are quite willing to make near-term investments that reduce a company's long-term cost structure to improve its future leverage. They are fully prepared to underwrite the transition expenses associated with data center consolidation programs, staff relocation plans, outsourcing projects, and vendor replacement initiatives if such steps significantly reduce future IT spending. Some IT leaders suffer from such a myopic focus on achieving near-term cost savings that they fail to propose more fundamental initiatives that could significantly modify IT's historical spending patterns. The majority of CFOs are more than ready to entertain discussions of multiyear spending initiatives if such initiatives can improve their company's long-term leverage.

Sound financial management ultimately relies on timely and accurate financial information. Most corporate finance groups assign a financial analyst to the IT organization. This individual plays a key role in constructing the annual budget and in tracking variances against approved spending plans. In most instances, IT groups need additional financial support to construct reliable business cases for major initiatives, perform project-level accounting on major spending programs, prepare bottom-up capital spending plans, determine the total cost of ownership of selected systems and services, examine trade-offs between internal and external cloud infrastructure investments, etc. The financial analysts assigned to IT typically don't have the time or IT experience required to perform these types of activities. IT groups can bolster the integrity of their financial management practices by establishing a small team of internal business analysts who can provide the granular information that is ultimately required to make informed financial decisions. One or two competent individuals performing these roles can have a remarkable impact on the financial credibility of the entire IT organization.

The Chargeback Trap

Chargeback systems are designed to allocate IT expenses to specific functions or business units within a company. Showback systems serve a similar purpose, however they merely attribute costs to functions or units without triggering internal accounting transfers of corporate funds.

Chargeback systems have a hypnotic appeal to IT leaders. Many CIO forums reserve time for spontaneous roundtable discussions of recent accomplishments or activities within each CIO's organization. If one of the participants announces that she has recently implemented a chargeback system, you can immediately shelve the remaining portions of the agenda. The chargeback discussion will take center stage for the remainder of the meeting.

The interest in chargeback systems is extremely well intended but unfortunately misplaced. In theory, more accurate information about the level of spending required to support different functions and business units should influence future demand for IT services. Larger functions and more profitable units should logically have the resources required to procure more sophisticated services. In practice, however, it's extremely difficult to restrict the scope or quality of IT services on a functional or business unit basis. For example: Should the marketing team be given access to better, faster business intelligence (BI) capabilities to manage marketing campaigns during the Christmas shopping season than the procurement team which needs similar capabilities to manage the company's global supply chain? Should the major offices of a less profitable subsidiary be supplied with lower capacity network circuits than those of a more profitable business unit? Should the email inboxes of a less profitable division be sized differently from those of a more profitable division?

Even if it were technically possible to differentiate the scope or quality of IT services among various functions and units, as a practical matter it's culturally and politically impossible to do so. Employees have a near-religious conviction that they have an inalienable right to the best IT services their companies can afford. They rarely tolerate discriminatory support practices. (Clearly, there are some exceptions to this principle. Financial services employees involved in stock or currency trading will invariably receive IT capabilities that are clearly superior to those of their colleagues in other divisions.)

Consequently, the theoretical belief that improved understanding of IT costs will reduce user demands and ultimately reduce IT spending is speculative at best and rarely substantiated. This would be true even if IT costs could be perfectly allocated to individual units and functions. However, that's the second major flaw of chargeback systems: they rely on a series of assumptions that are largely subjective in nature. Relatively modest changes to a few of these assumptions can produce markedly different allocation results. There is no such thing as a fair or accurate chargeback system. Fairness or accuracy is determined purely in the eye of the beholder, and in a large corporation there are a lot of beholders!

To illustrate this problem, consider a company that employs a legacy mainframe system to support its customer billing and payment processing activities. Assume that two divisions within the company use the same mainframe system for this purpose. The less profitable division transacts business in much smaller increments, relying upon a large number of transactions which each have a relatively small dollar value. The more profitable division employs far fewer transactions which each have a much higher dollar value. So what's the fairest way of apportioning the mainframe's expenses between these two divisions? The mainframe is sized on the basis of the number of total transactions that must be supported. The mainframe doesn't know the difference between a $5,000 transaction and a $500,000 transaction. If the mainframe costs were apportioned on a transaction basis, the less profitable division would carry the bigger charge, effectively subsidizing the use of the mainframe by the more profitable division. On the other hand, if the mainframe costs were apportioned on the basis of the total dollar value of the transactions managed for each division, the more profitable division would end up subsidizing the higher transaction flow of its less profitable counterpart. What constitutes a fair basis for allocating mainframe expenses in this situation?

Don't be fooled by claims that cost chargeback systems can be easily constructed. It takes considerable effort to compile the information needed to place costs in specific "buckets" and determine the fairest basis for allocating each bucket. The scope and size of individual service buckets are frequently debated ad nauseum, and political considerations play a major role in determining the fairest allocation metrics. Even after a final compromise has been reached regarding cost classifications and allocation metrics, it will be quite easy for a disinterested third party to suggest alternative classifications and metrics that would result in significantly different chargeback results.

It's Still Too Much!

Contrary to the advice provided in this chapter, I was foolhardy enough to construct a chargeback system during the early stages of my career. IT expenses were divided among fourteen different services. The total cost of each service was subsequently allocated to five different operating divisions. Individual service categories included such things as telecom connectivity, the ERP system, the data warehouse, the mainframe, desktop computing capabilities, etc. The IT charges for each division were adjusted on an annual basis to reflect anticipated changes in service delivery costs during the coming year and divisional usage levels during the prior year. I personally presented a customized forecast of divisional IT costs to each divisional president during the annual budgeting process. At the conclusion of one of these briefings, the president of the largest operating division said, "I understand how you constructed my bill for next year and I understand the basis for the cost increases you've highlighted, but *it still feels as if I'm paying too much for IT* and you've got to find a way of decreasing my IT expenses!" So after all the work involved in constructing an itemized bill describing the support costs for his division, I had still failed to convince him that his IT expenses were fair and reasonable. Bottom line: just because you present people with data, you can't always change the way they feel!

In summary, chargeback initiatives should not be initiated casually or with the vague intention of providing more cost transparency for the IT function. They inevitably require significantly more effort than originally anticipated. Their results can be easily altered or manipulated by slight modifications to cost classifications or allocation metrics. And finally, their results are unlikely to lead to significant changes in IT demand for a variety of cultural and political reasons.

IT leaders should also evaluate the opportunity costs associated with chargeback systems. Couldn't all the organizational time and effort that goes into the construction of a chargeback system be better used elsewhere to improve IT performance and bolster IT credibility? Chargeback discussions with business leaders frequently beg more questions than they answer and rarely achieve the cost transparency that was initially desired. Many such discussions degenerate into contentious debates regarding the scope, quality, and necessity of IT services. Most business executives hold strong personal convictions about the cost effectiveness of their IT organizations, but their convictions are frequently based on anecdotal experiences and not on the integrity of the chargeback bill they receive from IT. Personal perceptions will trump hard data almost every time IT costs are under discussion!

Industry consultants have suggested that a more useful way of discussing costs with business executives is to differentiate expenses required to run the business on a daily basis from other expenses that are designed to grow or transform current business operations. More specifically, run-the-business expenses are defined as those costs required to maintain current operations with no significant improvements in the functionality or quality of existing IT services. Grow-the-business investments are incremental expenditures that enhance, extend, or expand current IT capabilities. Transform-the-business expenditures are associated with major initiatives that result in new strategic IT capabilities.

Unfortunately, as is the case with chargeback systems, there are no standard industry classifications of run/grow/transform expenses beyond the broad conceptual definitions provided above. A transformational expense in one company might be a growth expense in another. For example, the first insurance company to build a mobile application for managing customer claims would undoubtedly classify the application's development and support costs as transformational in nature. When the last of its competitors develops a similar application, are such costs still transformational or are they simply required to grow the business in a fashion that's consistent with current customer expectations?

Tracking and reporting run/grow/transform expenses on an annual basis is likely to be another high effort–low return activity that will be highly subjective in nature and have only marginal value in justifying IT expenditures. It could, in fact, backfire if business leaders don't attribute any business significance to the run/grow/transform categories. Under these circumstances, tracking and reporting IT costs within the run/grow/transform framework is an exercise in organizational narcissism, performed primarily for the entertainment of IT management.

Although chargeback systems frequently generate little value at the cost of considerable effort, there are selected situations in which they serve a useful financial purpose, such as the following:

- Large corporations commonly establish IT shared-service organizations to achieve economies of scale in their daily IT operations and improve their negotiating leverage with major suppliers. Centralized shared-service organizations routinely use chargeback systems to allocate costs to individual operating divisions. Many such organizations have existed for years, or even decades, and their chargeback schemes have become fully institutionalized. Under these circumstances, the financial benefits of operating scale and negotiating leverage far outweigh any potential inequities in the ways that IT costs are being allocated.

- Large corporations may seek to report the profitability of their subsidiaries or divisions on an individual basis and consequently apportion some or all of their centrally incurred IT costs to individual operating entities. IT costs are frequently allocated to divisions being targeted for future divestiture to ensure that prospective buyers have an accurate understanding of the division's true operating expenses.

- Some corporations seek to minimize G&A expenses by apportioning selected IT expenditures to other P&L line item categories such as sales and marketing or R&D.

- In some instances, there may be tax advantages associated with allocating IT costs to business units or operations that are based outside North America.

In summary, there are situations in which IT cost-allocation schemes are beneficial, but in most situations the benefits are purely financial in nature. Any improvements in IT cost transparency or demand management achieved through these measures are mostly coincidental and rarely significant.

If the construction of a chargeback system becomes politically inescapable, it's best to start small and evolve over time. Don't attempt to include all current IT costs in the first version of the system. Start with services whose costs and allocation metrics are easy to identify, such as PC, smartphone, and service desk support. Incorporate additional services in subsequent fiscal years with the long-term goal of eventually allocating 80 percent or more of the total IT budget. To the maximum extent possible, enlist the participation of functional or business unit executives in defining the chargeback service catalog and validating the allocation metrics proposed for individual services. Business participation in the construction of chargeback systems is crucially important if they are to serve any useful purpose in rationalizing IT expenses.

Chapter 2

Get Them to Like You

IT leaders can contribute to the financial success of their companies in three principal ways. They can focus on the internal workings of the IT organization and improve its efficiency and effectiveness. They can join forces with business leaders and leverage IT capabilities to improve the efficiency and effectiveness of their company's business processes. Finally, in relatively rare circumstances, they find ways of enabling strategic initiatives that yield transformative business results in terms of market expansion, customer retention, average transaction value, and the like.

Admittedly, there may be other paths to value creation. Some IT organizations host the systems that customers employ to purchase a company's products and access its services. They deliver tremendous value by ensuring that revenue-generating systems are available and highly responsive on a 24×7 basis. In other circumstances, IT organizations may assume broader responsibilities for their company's information security needs, business continuity plans, or supply chain operations. Obviously, there are additional paths to value creation when the role of the IT organization expands beyond its conventional boundaries.

The internal path to value creation is almost wholly under the control of the IT leader. He can explore a variety of ways to streamline IT procedures, reduce IT costs, restructure IT teams, improve interactions with business clients, etc. Many IT leaders instinctively focus their attention on internal value creation because the cost and mechanics of internal work processes are relatively well understood; best practices learned in one IT organization can be readily adapted for reuse elsewhere; and changes to existing practices can be made largely on a unilateral basis without the formal concurrence of external stakeholders.

The second path to value creation requires partnership with business leaders. The second path focuses on critical business processes such as lead generation, sales territory management, inventory velocity, order fulfillment, invoicing and cash collection, etc. IT cannot independently reengineer a company's business processes. Business process changes can only be achieved through close collaboration with business leaders, and close collaboration can only be achieved if constructive working relationships have been established with such leaders.

Members of the IT organization who work closely with business teams commonly encounter significant inefficiencies in current business practices. As technologists, they're convinced that changes to existing systems could reduce or eliminate many such inefficiencies. They become extremely frustrated when their suggestions are ignored and instinctively blame business leaders for being too stupid or too distracted to address the chronic process issues they've observed. These technologists would be shocked to learn that many business leaders share their concerns but have no desire to work with IT on potential improvements because they lack faith in IT's ability to deliver tangible results on time and on budget. A lack of mutual trust and respect between business leaders and their IT counterparts will severely limit, if not eliminate, IT's ability to generate value through business process reengineering.

The transformative path to value creation is a much higher risk–reward proposition. It usually involves a significant investment of funds, potential organizational changes, and a wholesale reprioritization of existing business initiatives. Transformative initiatives are not undertaken lightly and typically require the endorsement of a company's CEO, CFO, and one or more business unit leaders. If IT leaders seek to play a material role in planning these types of initiatives, they must exhibit a high degree of business intelligence and be trusted as seasoned business executives, not just technical leaders.

Of the three paths described above, the only one that is wholly under the control of an IT leader is the first: improving the efficiency and effectiveness of the IT organization itself. Substantive changes to a company's current business processes can only be achieved if business leaders trust IT to deliver the application and infrastructure capabilities required to support such changes. Substantive involvement in transformative initiatives requires an even higher degree of trust and collaboration on business outcomes, not just technical specifications.

Leaders who fail to develop effective working relationships with their business counterparts will find their ability to contribute to their company's financial success severely curtailed. Their primary—maybe exclusive—focus will be on the efficiency and effectiveness of the IT organization. IT organizations whose principal means of generating value is through internal restructuring, budget cuts, and staffing reductions are suffering from a wholesale failure of IT leadership. The only viable breakout strategy for such organizations is to initiate intentional campaigns to improve communication and collaboration with key business leaders. Trusted relationships are the ultimate litmus test of IT–business alignment, a concept that is widely referenced but poorly understood within most companies.

Relationship Building Is Job One

Newly appointed CIOs typically conduct All Hands meetings with their teams shortly after assuming their new positions. Such meetings are usually short on substance. A new CIO frankly doesn't know enough about her new organization or the company's business challenges to offer a concrete plan for the future of the IT group. The introductory All Hands meeting is primarily an opportunity for the CIO to describe her past work experience, establish her competence in the eyes of the group, and dispel any rumors that she is the devil incarnate!

I held such a meeting shortly after assuming a new CIO role several years ago. I did my best to pass along positive comments regarding the performance of the IT team that I'd obtained through initial interactions with my fellow executives. I also did my best to avoid any comments that might trigger unnecessary anxieties regarding changes to existing organizational structures, project priorities, vendor relationships, etc. In other words, I delivered an innocuous set of remarks that were politically correct and completely noncommittal, then I solicited questions from the group.

After several moments of painful silence, someone in the back of the room stood up and humored me by asking, "Now that you've been here for four weeks, what's the first thing you plan to do?" I replied, "I intend to spend most of my time with the other executives and try to get them to like me." My answer brought the house down. Everyone laughed. When I met with my direct reports immediately after the meeting, they congratulated me on such an amusing response. I told them it was sincere and based upon previous experience. Things go wrong all the time within IT. If your customers like you, they'll forgive a world of sins. If they don't, they'll kill you!

Common Mistakes in Business Relationship Management

Collaborative relationships between IT leaders and their business counterparts may be difficult to initiate and even more difficult to sustain for a variety of reasons. Some of the more common pitfalls are listed below. This is not a prioritized list, nor is it exhaustive.

Mistake No. 1: Focusing on Form over Substance

Many IT leaders assume that constructive relationships are a natural consequence of frequent communication. Therefore, they establish a series of formal activities to institutionalize communication with their business counterparts. With the best of intentions, IT leaders organize oversight committees to approve IT investments, conduct service reviews with key business executives, provide regular updates on the progress of major projects, solicit input on business needs in advance of the annual budgeting process, assign relationship managers to major business units, etc. Business leaders commonly lose interest in such activities or their participation is preempted by more urgent business concerns. A great deal of staff time is invested in supporting these types of activities but they often fail to change deep-seated convictions about the competence or trustworthiness of the IT team.

Mistake No. 2: Emphasizing Analysis over Intuition

IT leaders commonly have highly developed analytical skills established through years of formal training and on-the-job experience. Many business leaders lack formal training in science or engineering and rarely become personally involved in the planning or conduct of analytical exercises. They delegate those activities to their staff and focus their attention on the results or outcomes of such studies. Seasoned business executives have a strong tendency to base decisions on intuition, whereas their IT counterparts continue to rely on analytical studies to justify many, if not most, of their decisions.

This is not to suggest that business decisions in large, multibillion-dollar enterprises are based on the whims or personal preferences of senior executives. Significant analysis is required to arrive at any major business decision. But the contrast between the skills and decision-making tendencies of business and IT leaders easily leads to situations in which they "talk past" each other and fail to communicate effectively.

An IT leader may feel compelled to explain the data and analytical procedures that provide the basis for his decision while his business counterpart is yearning to get to the proverbial "bottom line" of their conversation. Conversely, a business executive may explain a decision to his IT counterpart in terms of past personal experiences that are far too qualitative to satisfy the instinctive analytical needs of his IT listener. IT leaders need to gauge the decision-making needs of business leaders very carefully to ensure they are speaking a common language and to avoid excessive staff work on analytical studies that are totally unnecessary.

Mistake No. 3: Settling for One-Dimensional Relationships

IT leaders have a tendency to interact with their business counterparts on an "as needed" basis. They schedule meetings with business leaders to discuss specific topics. It would never occur to them to schedule an unstructured one-on-one meeting with no predetermined agenda. Nor would they be inclined to spontaneously interrupt or disturb an executive who was alone in his office. They would simply assume that such an interruption was unwelcome or unwarranted because that's the way they would react if someone interrupted them. These types of relationships are one dimensional. They are based on business need and are wholly transactional in nature. In contrast, other leaders in the company engage in unstructured and spontaneous conversations all the time. Furthermore, they use such interactions to develop a social dimension in their relationships with one another.

The most effective working relationships in business are two dimensional, and have both a social and a business component. The social dimension is actually the easiest to cultivate. Most individuals telegraph their outside-of-work interests rather openly and require very little urging to talk about their kids, their favorite sports teams, the colleges they attended, their vacations and hobbies, etc. It's actually difficult to *not* find some type of common outside-of-work interest that can form the basis of a social relationship with a business colleague.

How About Them Yankees?

One of the most effective working relationships I developed with a CFO was based upon a common interest (obsession?) with the New York Yankees. The CFO and I were the first two executives to arrive at the office on most workdays. We inevitably found ourselves in the break room every morning, by ourselves, getting our first cup of coffee. Invariably, one of us would express elation or disdain over some aspect of the previous night's Yankees game. We would banter on about a great hit, an unfair call, or a spectacular catch for five to ten minutes before returning to our desks to start work. That investment of five or ten minutes during the baseball season paid major dividends during the fall budgeting season. The CFO consistently treated me as a business peer instead of an order-taking subordinate, based in part on our mutual affection for the Yankees. I was able to negotiate the IT spending target for the following year with minimal posturing or gamesmanship because of the personal relationship we had established together.

The business dimension of a working relationship is more important and more difficult to construct. IT leaders need to exhibit both general and specific business knowledge to establish their business credibility. General knowledge is typically acquired over time by working within a series of companies or operating divisions with widely varying business models, competitive challenges, and growth opportunities. Specific knowledge of the issues and opportunities confronting an individual executive can only be obtained by spending time with that executive and key members of his team.

A genuine curiosity about how a business works is one of the most important traits of successful IT leaders. Business executives cannot fail to be impressed when their IT counterparts proactively seek opportunities to learn about their problems and challenges. Much can be learned by attending regularly scheduled reviews, seeking invitations to strategy meetings, or spending time at work locations where an executive's team is concentrated. Even if the IT leader's ability to participate in such meetings is limited by his lack of domain knowledge, he will nevertheless score points by dedicating time to such activities and will inevitably improve his knowledge in the process. The fact that no IT leader has asked to attend a quarterly business review or sales strategy session or customer meeting in the past does not mean that your participation would be unwelcome (although it may take your business counterpart a few seconds to overcome her initial surprise at your expression of interest!).

Business travel is the ultimate petri dish for cultivating IT-business relationships. There's ample downtime during a business trip to casually share out-of-office interests, and there are multiple opportunities for participating in substantive business discussions, both formally and informally. Some of the most valuable lessons regarding the issues and opportunities facing your company can be learned in airline lounges or over business dinners rather than in formal conference rooms. Invitations to travel with business peers or join them for lunch or dinner should never be casually declined.

Mistake No. 4: Failing to Make Regular Deposits in the Relationship Bank

IT leaders should never, ever find themselves in a position where they are meeting an influential business executive for the first time to ask for forgiveness or to ask for money! As obvious as this may seem, few IT leaders appreciate the importance of establishing a positive balance in the emotional bank accounts they maintain with their business peers. Positive balances are absolutely essential to withstand the "withdrawals" that are required when apologizing for operational mistakes or seeking support for new initiatives.

If an IT leader is meeting an executive for the first time to explain an operational blunder or seek funding for an IT initiative, he is essentially dealing with a total stranger who has zero emotional empathy for the leader's dilemma or agenda. In either of these situations, the IT leader is asking the executive to "trust me" that the operational snafu has been fixed and will never occur again, or to "trust me" that the funds being solicited will yield meaningful business benefits. If the existing relationship between these two individuals is superficial or nonexistent, there's really no basis for the executive to trust the leader's promises.

Relationship management is ultimately an exercise in time management. Successful IT leaders consciously and intentionally devote time to cultivating relationships with business counterparts whose guidance and support can yield the greatest benefits for themselves and their organizations. Productive two-dimensional relationships need to be nurtured though frequent face-to-face contact, which can be spontaneous, casual, or structured in nature. The easiest time to build a positive cash balance in a financial bank account is when withdrawals are not required. The same holds true in establishing a positive emotional balance in the relationships that IT leaders establish with their business peers.

A Simple Test of Your Relationship Management Priorities

Draw a vertical line down the center of a piece of paper. To the left of the center line, list every peer or superior in the IT organization with whom you spoke during the past one to two weeks. Interactions in large group meetings don't count. List only those individuals you spoke with directly in one-on-one conversations, regardless of the length or subject matter of the conversations. To the right of the center line, list all business representatives you conversed with over the same period of time who hold positions that are comparable or superior to yours in the company hierarchy. If the ratio of internal conversations to external conversations exceeds 3:1 you need to start taking some business colleagues to lunch!

Ironically, some of the deepest and strongest IT–business relationships are forged during times of crisis, when a major IT initiative is on the verge of failure or adverse business conditions require significant reductions in IT spending. Although effective, lasting relationships can be formed under these circumstances, they require extraordinary effort to overcome any latent disrespect, distrust, or cynicism that may have developed through past dealings. The effort required to establish constructive working relationships under normal business conditions is quite modest by comparison, and can generate a tremendous return on the personal time invested, especially in times of crisis.

Mistake No. 5: Being Poisoned by Your Own Team

In a strange and somewhat counterintuitive way, the leader's own organization may lobby against her relationship-building efforts. Business relationship managers, service managers, or business systems analysts may feel it's their responsibility to deal with business representatives. If they believe their leader is devoting too much of her personal time to building business relationships, they may feel that their organizational roles are being co-opted or diminished in significance. Alternatively, relationship managers and business analysts may have become so frustrated by their inability to establish effective relationships with their business counterparts that they may advise their leader to abandon her outreach efforts altogether because they are doomed to fail.

Customer-First Leadership

IT leaders could take a lesson from the relationship-building priorities of seasoned CEOs. When a new CEO arrives at a corporation, the leader of every business unit and functional group queues up for time on his schedule. They all want to describe the importance of their respective organizations, the challenges and opportunities they face, and the strategies they are currently pursuing. A newly appointed CEO will also be encouraged to tour the company's major offices to reassure employees about the continuity of current operations and to share his vision regarding the company's growth prospects. New CEOs who follow this script won't get around to meeting major customers until they've been on the job for ninety days or more.

Seasoned CEOs typically have other priorities when they assume new CEO positions. Many will limit the number of internal reviews and employee meetings they conduct during their first sixty days on the job in order to spend time with customers. Customers invariably provide direct and unvarnished feedback about the utility and quality of the company's products that may be difficult to discern from internal briefings. Customers will also provide insight into the ease of doing business with the CEO's company, or the lack thereof. This external perspective is invaluable in the CEO's initial dealings with members of his own team. It severely limits his team's ability to blame the company's failings on the unrealistic demands or inexplicable behaviors of its customers!

IT leaders would profit from adopting similar relationship-building priorities upon assuming new roles. IT organizations are primarily service organizations. They support the units and functions that develop products and deal with customers. They cannot directly generate income or profit themselves. IT's success is ultimately determined by the leaders of the units and functions they support. Direct feedback from these business leaders is essential to the success of any IT leader. Indirect feedback through members of his own team is not sufficient and may actually be misleading.

Mistake No. 6: Building Relationships That Are Easy Instead of Those That Count

Not all business units and functions are created equally. This is a primary rule of office politics. There's an inevitable pecking order in the importance of a corporation's units and functions that usually corresponds to the financial results they deliver. Individual companies may develop cultures that are dominated by one or two functions, such as sales, marketing, engineering, or manufacturing. Others may be dominated by the needs or desires of their top-grossing operating divisions. In either situation, certain business leaders will have more influence and impact on strategic decisions than others. Astute IT leaders will apportion their relationship-building time and attention accordingly. More effort may be required to establish effective relationships with the leaders of dominant business units or influential functions but such efforts will yield disproportionate benefits when major decisions impacting IT are under consideration.

IT Staff Members Need to Like You, Too!

The forgoing discussion has focused exclusively on the benefits of establishing effective working relationships with business leaders. An equally important set of relationships needs to be cultivated within the IT team itself. External relationships can only be maintained when the IT group delivers on its commitments to its business partners. Consistent delivery can only be achieved when an IT group follows its leadership. It's a lot easier for a group to follow leaders they like and respect than ones they dislike and suspect!

The relationships an IT leader establishes with her direct reports and team members are also two dimensional in nature. One dimension is social and follows the same general outlines as the social dimension of the business partner relationships discussed above. The other dimension is related to career development and advancement. IT staff members rely on their leaders to broaden their skills through training, special assignments, and periodic rotation into new positions. They seek assurances that their performance will be equitably rewarded through pay increases, bonuses, and promotions. They also seek evidence that their leaders understand their personal aspirations and are providing the performance feedback and developmental opportunities needed to compete for future career opportunities.

Discussions of career development issues in large group meetings or related announcements via email are useful and necessary, but direct personal discussions of career ambitions with current and emerging leaders are a much more tangible means of acknowledging career development concerns. Leaders of large organizations obviously don't have the time to meet individually with all of the members of their teams. However, the simple investment of time in career discussions with targeted individuals who are recognized as internal leaders will have a pronounced ripple effect on the broader organization. Individuals participating in these discussions will relay your personal commitment to career development to their peers and team members, and are more likely to hold similar conversations with members of their own teams as well.

Spending more one-on-one time with key staff members is a laudable leadership goal that few would contest. However, conducting such conversations on an ongoing basis requires deliberate time management. Career development discussions do not need to be long or complicated or critical in nature. They can easily be conducted while congratulating individuals on their recent performance or accomplishments. The trust, motivation, and enthusiasm engendered by such conversations can be quite large relative to the time invested.

It's hard to build a positive reputation outside the IT organization if you don't have one internally. A willingness to discuss outside-of-work interests and a commitment to career development are leadership traits that are universally admired in every IT shop. Once the team realizes that you are human and committed to their success—not just your own—they will follow you almost anywhere.

Chapter 3

Fishing in the Talent Pool

Everyone knows that the three critical ingredients for the success of any business venture are people, process, and technology—in that order. Professional sport franchises adhere religiously to this success formula. They aggressively recruit the best athletes they can afford. They establish rigorous training regimens and hone their players' skills through personal workouts, repetitive drills, and team practices. They build state-of-the-art weight rooms and training facilities. They develop customized nutrition programs for individual team members. They continually refine their playbooks. And they employ sophisticated analytical tools to dissect the tendencies and weaknesses of their opponents. In short, they invest in the people, processes, and technologies that give them the greatest chance of winning.

Success in major league sports starts and ends with the athletes on the team. No matter how smart the coaches are, no matter how clever the playbook is, no matter how much money was invested in the training facility or nutrition plans, success is ultimately determined by the athletes on the field of play. Irrespective of their training or leadership, the athletes are ultimately responsible for executing the game plan and mustering the grit and intelligence required to overcome their opponents. Success is not predicated solely on the athleticism or intelligence of individual players but on their collective ability to pool their talents and perform as a team.

The same critical success factors apply to IT organizations. However, IT managers tend to prioritize these factors in exactly the opposite order. They devote inordinate attention to selecting and implementing the technologies needed to conduct daily operations. They place less emphasis on refining internal processes and practices. And, last but not least, they concern themselves with recruiting, training, and deploying staff members in ways that will optimize the overall effectiveness of their organizations. Talent considerations are the number-one priority in building a successful sports franchise but they are frequently a third-order priority in building an effective IT organization.

It's difficult for IT groups to achieve compelling business advantages from their technology decisions or work processes because most groups have equal access to best-of-breed technology products and industry-leading operational practices. Technology vendors are constantly advertising their wares through emails, webinars, white papers, sales calls, and conference presentations. Consultants are equally anxious to assist organizations in improving the maturity of key internal processes such as project management (PMI), software development (Agile), service management (ITIL), or system operations (DevOps). If technology and management practices are equally available to all IT organizations, the only true source of competitive differentiation is the talent of the IT team.

Athletic talent is more than just physical ability and the knowledge of a particular sport. It's the ability to execute plays in a disciplined manner as well as the ability to improvise when necessary. It's the ability to adapt a game plan to adverse playing conditions, game day injuries, and the unanticipated tactics of competitors. It's the ability to establish amicable social relationships with teammates in the clubhouse and synergistic work relationships with teammates on the playing field.

It's the mental fortitude and emotional maturity to stay focused and keep playing when things don't go exactly as planned.

IT talent is also more than just knowledge and skills. It's the ability to enforce processes in a disciplined manner and not just design them. It's the ability to obtain the maximum benefit from technology investments and not just extract the best contractual terms from vendors. It's the ability to take calculated risks, learn from mistakes, and collaborate with coworkers in ways that make the entire team better. Talented teams enjoy working together. They continually learn from one another and have a deeply shared commitment to continuous performance improvement. They hold themselves accountable for results—both individually and collectively—without fear of reprisal or recrimination.

All IT managers pay homage to the importance of talent management. And yet, despite its universally recognized importance, few managers consistently devote time to defining their talent needs, prioritizing their talent gaps, and taking the steps needed to upgrade the talent mix of their teams.

Talent management is not a series of annual events devoted to performance reviews, succession planning, or career development. It's a coaching mentality that effective leaders employ to maximize the output and impact of their team members. Talent management occurs every day in the casual words of praise that are bestowed or withheld from individual team members. It occurs in the decisions that are made about work assignments, meeting participation, presentation opportunities, interoffice travel, and task prioritization. Talent management should be a conscious agenda item on the weekly activity calendar of every IT manager. Time should be set aside explicitly to provide feedback and suggestions on current assignments, discuss career aspirations, deliver well-earned compliments, and ensure that training opportunities are being properly leveraged. Talent management is far too important to be consistently overshadowed by the operational issues, project management concerns, budget problems, and vendor briefings that fill the calendars of most IT managers.

The Hand You've Been Dealt

One of the primary reasons IT managers devote so little attention to talent management is that it's difficult to make changes to existing teams. The processes required to eliminate individuals on the basis of their personal performance or eliminate positions through job restructuring are cumbersome and time consuming. Employee terminations and job restructuring inevitably unleash a wave of anxiety within an organization that can impede or undermine other initiatives. It's equally difficult to redeploy existing talent. Using existing staff members to plug talent gaps in one part of the organization frequently creates gaps elsewhere with no net gain in overall efficiency or effectiveness. For all of these reasons, managers assigned to new roles have a reflexive tendency to initially focus on their budgets, principal customers, and major projects. Talent assessment appears on the to-do list of any newly assigned manager, but it rarely rises to the top of the list.

Perceptions regarding the talents of individual IT teams or team members can be strongly influenced by their affiliation with specific groups or departments. These affiliations trigger subliminal notions about an individual's technical abilities, interpersonal skills, or change capacity that can be misleading or completely erroneous. The most common preconceived notions regarding an individual's capabilities are triggered by his technical background, service tenure, acquisition history, and local work environment. Preconceived notions can be readily overcome by personal experience but any newly appointed manager will invariably use affiliations—either consciously or subconsciously—to size up the talent on her team. In effect, these affiliations tend to compartmentalize talent and frequently cloud a manager's judgment regarding the sophistication and scalability of her existing human resources.

Technical Background

The skills, responsibilities, and work cultures of application and infrastructure teams differ significantly. Application teams have direct and frequent contact with business representatives. Consequently, they develop a keen appreciation of current business issues and priorities. They commonly support a variety of concurrent projects and become adept at managing the ebb and flow of project work. In contrast, infrastructure teams have fewer direct contacts with business representatives. They provide ongoing operational support for critical business systems and typically adopt a more hierarchical command-and-control approach to managing their daily activities. The growing adoption of DevOps procedures may blur the divisions between applications and infrastructure teams in some newer, smaller companies but their contrasting behaviors are an inescapable fact of life in large enterprises managing complex portfolios of legacy systems.

Perceptions regarding the capabilities of individuals within these two teams are invariably tainted by the stereotypical work profiles presented above. Application managers are commonly considered to be too undisciplined to manage the stringent operational requirements of business-critical systems. Conversely, infrastructure managers would rarely be considered for application leadership roles because they presumably lack the influencing skills needed to work effectively with business representatives. Irrespective of whether such prejudices are true or false in any given situation, they inevitably form a subliminal lens that managers employ in handing out assignments and targeting training opportunities.

Service Tenure

Unfortunately, many IT groups suffer from an "old guard" versus "new guard" mentality. The old guard consists of long-term employees with service tenures of ten years or greater. These individuals possess a deep understanding of legacy systems and infrastructure. They've experienced the wrath of business partners when things have gone wrong in the past. Consequently, they have a deep intuitive appreciation of systems and capabilities that are truly business critical. The new guard consists of employees with service tenures of five years or less. Even if they're not new college graduates, they've come from other environments where they've been exposed to different business processes, technologies, support systems, and operational practices. They inevitably seek to introduce some of the capabilities they've experienced elsewhere into their current organizations.

In many IT shops, the tenure demographics of the team are distinctly bimodal, with a clear cluster of old timers, a prominent group of newcomers, and relatively few in-betweeners to bridge the gap. Ideally, the old timers and newcomers should appreciate the unique skills and experiences they each possess and actively seek to learn from one another. In practice, this is rarely the case. The two groups tend to become openly disrespectful of one another's technical abilities and blatantly critical of each other's relevance to the future success of the team.

Once again, perceptions regarding individuals can be strongly influenced by their affiliation with the old guard versus the new guard. New guard employees are commonly perceived to be more aggressive change agents while old guard employees are presumed to be change resistant. Ironically, old guard employees may have far more experience implementing major IT initiatives within the unique cultures of their companies than their new guard colleagues, even though they're publicly considered to be obstacles to change.

Acquisition History

Almost all major enterprises employ acquisition strategies to expand the size and scope of their business. IT organizations grow through this process as well, frequently absorbing talent from newly acquired companies. In some instances, acquired staff members may bring unique knowledge about new technologies or operational procedures that can directly benefit the acquiring organization. In other cases, the acquirees may lack the technical knowledge and business expertise that is required to succeed in their new environments.

The disparity in skills and experience within teams built through acquisition can be particularly acute when "big company" IT teams inherit talent from significantly smaller organizations. Multibillion-dollar companies operate quite differently from multimillion-dollar companies. IT shops in big companies typically procure applications, hardware, and services from first-tier vendors. They make extensive use of consultants and contractors to plug critical skill gaps on a temporary basis. Their decision-making processes are inherently more cumbersome because of their sheer size, complexity, and aversion to risk.

Individuals who were perceived to be IT leaders in small companies may struggle to make the transition to big-company environments. In some cases, they may simply lack familiarity with more sophisticated technologies that are commonly employed in large enterprises. In other instances, the tactical focus, unilateral decision making, and take-charge behaviors that made them successful in a smaller organization may actually undermine their effectiveness in a big company where job responsibilities tend to be more specialized and interdisciplinary teamwork is essential.

The upward potential of team members inherited through small company acquisitions needs to be tested and validated. They may have significant technical blind spots in their experience and a bias toward tactical decision-making that limit their ability to assume broader leadership roles.

Local Environment

As companies expand the global scope of their business operations, IT organizations become increasingly global as well. Most IT shops in global enterprises maintain teams at multiple sites in North America, Europe, and Asia.

In the not-so-distant past, North American companies retained the majority of IT leadership roles within North America. Operations in other geographies were considered subordinate in nature and expected to take direction from the North American management team. Contemporary management teams are far more geographically dispersed. In today's environment, it's not at all uncommon for a data center operations team in North America to report to an individual in India or for an applications support team in North America to report to a leader in London.

Assessing the talent of individuals operating in different time zones and cultures can be very tricky. With limited face-to-face contact, it's difficult to ascertain how an individual spends his time or works with others. Local advancement criteria may be heavily influenced by cultural norms. Behaviors that might be prized and rewarded in one culture may be viewed as undesirable or disruptive in another.

While it's true that modern collaboration tools enable many geographically distributed teams to be productive, extra effort is required to evaluate the capabilities of individuals participating on such teams. The success that an individual achieves within a specific team—physical or virtual—may not be easily replicated within a different environment or assignment.

Managers start mentally classifying the capabilities of their team members on their first day in a new job, either consciously or subconsciously. Like it or not, they all suffer from a set of preconceived notions regarding the influence of technical background, service tenure, acquisition lineage, and local environments on each individual's abilities. Managers need to consciously acknowledge the existence of such notions and test them empirically to determine the true capabilities and potential of the team they've inherited.

Talent Debt Remediation

IT managers are painfully familiar with the concept of technical debt. This term was initially developed by software engineers to denote antiquated application architectures, programming languages, coding procedures, and embedded utilities that impede the incorporation of new functionality in legacy applications. Over time, the concept of technical debt has expanded to describe any set of technologies—software or hardware—that has become outmoded or obsolete. Technical debt can impose a tremendous drag on a team, increasing the cost, complexity, and risk associated with day-to-day operations. Efforts to remediate technical debt can divert time and attention from initiatives that produce more direct and immediate business benefits. Managers commonly bemoan the technical debt they've inherited when taking on new responsibilities, and they lobby aggressively for resources to replace outmoded capabilities.

Ironically, the technical debt that exists in most organizations extends deeply into the IT team as well. Talent debt can manifest itself in many different ways. It may manifest itself as a lack of knowledge or experience with contemporary technologies, a lack of discipline in adhering to operational procedures, a lack of teamwork, a lack of understanding about key business processes, a lack of financial management skills, or the inability to adapt to decision-making processes within a big-company environment. Although it's politically incorrect and probably counterproductive to openly lament the talent debt within an organization, talent debt can undermine the performance of an IT team in ways that are more pervasive and ultimately more damaging than technical debt.

IT leaders chip away at technical debt by developing long-term plans for replacing outmoded technologies. Some debt remediation programs are formal in nature and are funded as separate initiatives. Some are informal and conducted in conjunction with routine business-as-usual activities. In either case, managers focus their remediation efforts on systems or infrastructure capabilities that have the greatest business significance and are the most difficult to maintain and modify due to their antiquated components.

Technical remediation programs are designed to achieve a predetermined end state. Architects and engineers establish technical blueprints for aging systems that leverage the best aspects of a system's current design while incorporating modern technologies where possible and practicable. Individual system components are typically replaced in an incremental fashion until the targeted end-state design is actually achieved.

Similar strategies should be adopted in establishing remediation programs for an organization's talent debt. Most IT leaders have a keen appreciation of the future business demands that will be placed on their teams. They know the legacy skills that must be maintained to support legacy systems. They also appreciate the new skills that are needed to support their company's growth plans. These requirements should be used to establish staffing blueprints that are similar in nature to the technical blueprints referenced above.

Strategic staffing plans are not simply qualitative statements about skills that will become more or less important in the future. Nor are they lists of the next ten job requisitions that need to be opened when funding becomes available. Strategic staffing plans are explicit organizational blueprints describing future functional departments, job titles, and staffing levels. The contrast between a strategic staffing blueprint and a group's current organization chart will reveal critical talent deficiencies as well as critical talent surpluses.

IT leaders are frequently frustrated by the tactical nature of the hiring conducted within their organizations. The easiest way to justify additional head count is to embed it in business cases for major business initiatives or to appeal for emergency staff positions following a major calamity. (Everyone knows that the best time to request additional head count for the information security team is immediately after a major breach has occurred!) But in fairness to the CEOs and CFOs of most companies, CIOs actually perpetuate tactical recruiting practices by failing to present strategic staffing plans for executive discussion or approval. CIOs may request additional head count during the annual budgeting process and refer to such head count as strategic, but in the absence of an agreed-upon plan, how can any CEO or CFO be assured that the incremental positions being requested are truly strategic in nature?

Sooner or later, companies realize that the technical debt within their core IT systems is limiting their business agility, increasing their operating costs, and undermining the satisfaction of their customers. Technical debt can be retired through multiyear investments in legacy systems when such investments are justified in terms of accelerated product development, avoided support costs, or improved customer retention. Enlightened companies will make similar multiyear commitments to retiring talent debt when presented with carefully constructed staffing plans that are based on long-term business needs instead of short-term business exigencies.

Politically astute IT leaders divide staffing discussions with their executive colleagues into two sequential conversations. The first conversation is designed to reach agreement in principle on the future size, structure, and skill sets of the IT team. Vocal, emotional support from key client groups is essential in establishing executive consensus on this strategic blueprint. Blueprint conversations should be conducted outside the annual budgeting process, ideally at midyear when the annual competition for incremental funding has momentarily subsided. The second conversation should occur during the annual budgeting cycle. It serves as a reminder to executive leadership that this is their opportunity to make an installment payment on the staffing plan that was agreed upon six months earlier.

This logical, strategic approach to staffing doesn't carry a 100 percent guarantee of success. IT head count requests are easily trumped by more pressing business needs, depending upon the competitive pressures and growth opportunities facing individual companies. Nevertheless, the effort invested in achieving executive consensus about the current talent debt within the IT organization is more likely to pay future head count dividends than simply lurching from one tactical staffing request to the next.

It's not enough for CIOs to seek the commitment of their CEOs and CFOs to IT's strategic staffing plan. CIOs need to demonstrate their personal commitment to the plan as well. The CIO's direct reports need to be fully engaged in constructing such plans and fully committed to following their stated hiring priorities. Open positions created by voluntary employee departures should no longer be refilled automatically. All open head counts should be vetted against the priorities established in the strategic plan before being allocated to any specific team or department. Furthermore, the entire IT management team needs to take its performance management responsibilities very seriously. Individuals who fail to meet expectations need to be terminated and their head count needs to be recycled to address the more pressing strategic needs of the overall organization.

Business executives who believe that IT leaders have aligned their staffing plans with their company's growth strategies *and* who observe IT leaders proactively resolving the performance problems within their own organizations are far more likely to approve future investments in talent debt remediation.

Piecing Together the Leadership Puzzle

In principle, a group's organization chart should serve as a useful guide to its leaders. In a true meritocracy, individuals with superior technical talent, business intelligence, and collaboration skills should rise to positions of progressively greater responsibility and authority. In practice, merit-based advancement is rarely achieved consistently across an entire organization. Other factors such as unique skills, service tenure, personal relationships, and random luck can play a significant role in advancing individuals into the roles they occupy today.

It's rare for any one of these considerations to be a deciding factor in promotion decisions, but they collectively play a pervasive role in shaping the management hierarchy displayed on an organization chart. At best, the current chart is a fuzzy guide to individuals who possess the technical, business, and interpersonal skills needed to implement a new leader's agenda. At worst, it completely camouflages the latent talent within the organization. The following factors need to be considered in calibrating the capabilities of individuals who currently occupy leadership positions within the organization. Failure to account for these factors may lead to disastrous consequences if incumbent leaders are assigned to new roles for which they are wholly unsuited.

Unique Skills

Savantism is a rare condition in which people with developmental disorders possess one or more areas of expertise or brilliance that stand in sharp contrast to their broader emotional, intellectual, or behavioral disabilities. Savantism may be a rare condition outside IT organizations but it's actually quite common within them. Some individuals occupy positions of importance and authority simply because they know more about a particular topic than anyone else. IT savants are promoted into leadership positions based upon their deep technical knowledge, irrespective of their ability to manage people, finances, or business relationships. For example, the leader of the network engineering team may be a terrible people manager and incapable of operating within budget guidelines, but he remains the leader of the team because he's the only individual who truly understands the topology of the company's network. Similarly, the leader of the ERP support team may openly ridicule his peers and routinely ignore requests from his boss, but he has been allowed to survive in his leadership position because he's the only individual who truly understands the customizations that have been applied to the ERP system.

Service Tenure

Some individuals occupy positions of importance and authority simply because they outlasted their competitors and it was their turn to move up the hierarchy when a specific position became available. An individual promoted for this reason may not have been the most qualified candidate for his current role, but he may have been the longest-tenured candidate awaiting promotion within his former grade level.

There are clear advancement tracks in every IT organization. Service desk agents want to become application testers. Testers want to become developers. Developers want to become software engineers, and engineers want to become software architects. System administrators want to become operators, operators want to become system engineers, and engineers want to become system architects. Managers aspire to become senior managers, senior managers seek director positions, directors want to become senior directors, and so on. Everyone—either consciously or subconsciously—is monitoring time served in their current role and preparing to lobby for advancement if they feel they've been unfairly passed over. Management all too frequently yields to employee advancement demands simply to avoid conflict or conform to long-standing company traditions.

Personal Relationships

It's not always what you know, it's who you know! Ringing endorsements from business executives can play a big role in advancing the careers of IT professionals. To a degree, business endorsements should play a role in differentiating leaders who are technically competent *and* business savvy from others whose abilities are strictly technical in nature.

However, in some situations, business partner sponsorship can trump all other considerations and individuals advance within IT because business partners like them or trust them. The same phenomenon occurs within the IT organization itself. Individuals may be accelerated into positions for which they are not qualified simply because they are liked by a senior IT manager or respected for a single accomplishment.

Luck

It *is* better to be lucky than good! Some individuals occupy positions of authority simply because they were in the right place at the right time. For example, the leader of the network operations center may exhibit tremendous leadership during a major security breach and become the vice president of information security as a reward, even though his formal training in the security field is limited. Similarly, a company may seek an external candidate to serve as its first-ever chief data officer and end up promoting the existing leader of the data warehouse team into the job simply because no compelling external candidate could be identified.

Survival skills represent another form of luck. Some managers appear on the organization chart because they are serial survivors. They may not be the most talented or accomplished or well-liked members of the management team, but they have succeeded in moving around the organization frequently enough to avoid any consequences for their management deficiencies. Through sheer luck they've managed to avoid creating problems that would attract the attention of senior management and have changed roles frequently enough to avoid accountability for their lackluster performance. They commonly fill roles that are not considered to be critical or highly desirable. These individuals contribute little to the performance of the organization and block advancement opportunities for others.

Every IT leader needs to identify the individuals within his organization who can be relied upon to embrace his strategies, evangelize his initiatives and implement his agenda. The managers he inherits may possess many of the capabilities required for success but their positions on the current organization chart may be a poor guide to the roles they are best suited to play in the future.

Testing Your Talent

It's quite easy for IT leaders to misread or misinterpret the capabilities of their team members. As discussed above, leaders frequently develop preconceived notions about an individual's abilities based upon the individual's current role and responsibilities, her title or position, or her service tenure, work location, or past job experience. Leaders can also be misled by an individual's receptivity to change.

Existing staff members typically respond to new leaders in one of three ways. Roughly 20 percent of the existing team considers the new leader to be the "new messiah" who will correct all of the organization's woes. These individuals love change for change's sake and want to join the vanguard of any initiative the new leader proposes. At the other end of the spectrum, another 20 percent of the team views the new leader with deep skepticism, verging on cynicism. They either believe that the current state of affairs is perfectly fine and no changes are required, or they believe the organization is so dysfunctional that it's impossible to institute any type of permanent constructive change. The remaining 60 percent of the team are fence-sitters. They adopt a wait-and-see attitude to determine if the new leader's ideas will actually gain traction with senior management and key business partners.

New leaders have a natural tendency to embrace their instinctive followers and ignore their cynics. It's only natural to be attracted to like-minded individuals and reward their enthusiasm with leadership roles in the new world order being established by the leader. This can actually be quite dangerous. Naïve zealots may produce some early failures that can significantly derail the leader's change agenda. Even if the zealots are able to achieve some early successes, they may not command sufficient respect within the organization to influence the perspectives of their fence-sitting colleagues. On the other hand, converted cynics can have a huge impact on the perceptions of the broader organization. When fence sitters see cynics supporting a new leader's agenda they are far more likely to jump on the bandwagon and support it themselves.

The only way to truly evaluate the talent within an organization is to test it. New leaders should not be overly reliant on the historical reputations or past accomplishments of their team members. They should directly assess the capabilities and growth potential of key individuals by testing them. The leader has a wide variety of testing mechanisms at his disposal. Team members can be asked to perform specific studies, make presentations, take on special assignments, rotate into roles outside their areas of formal training, etc. The goal of such tests is not necessarily to requalify individuals for their current positions but to determine if they have the ability to assume broader, more strategic roles in the future.

Many leaders make the mistake of conducting tests that play to the known strengths of individuals. For example, an infrastructure manager who has been particularly adept at building annual budgets for his team may be asked to play a broader role in facilitating the annual budgeting process for the overall IT organization. Alternatively, an application manager who has developed a successful process for implementing quarterly enhancements to the company's ERP system may be asked to establish a similar process for making changes to the company's CRM system. In both of these hypothetical scenarios individuals are being asked to replicate their past success by leveraging their proven skills in a different context or domain.

Assignments that move individuals out of their established comfort zones and test their ability to develop new skills or rectify known weaknesses are far more revealing. For example, an individual with proven analytical skills could be placed in an assignment where his ability to influence external stakeholders is critical to success. Alternatively, a highly respected application development manager might be given an operational challenge, such as improving the first call resolution of issues submitted to the service desk.

The ultimate stretch assignment in IT is one that crosses the Great Divide that separates the application and infrastructure teams. Very few individuals are willing to cross the Divide and assume roles outside their areas of historical expertise, even on a temporary basis. However, those who do are frequently rewarded with a wider variety of advancement opportunities.

Rotational assignments across the Great Divide also benefit the broader IT organization. Not surprisingly, IT management teams that include individuals who have worked in applications and infrastructure are more effective because they develop a common understanding of the operational imperatives and success criteria that exist on both sides of the Divide. New leaders should actively seek out opportunities to evaluate the talent on their teams through assignments that bridge the Divide. Such assignments will benefit the participants and the broader IT organization.

The Paradox of Career Development

Career development is a chronic concern in all IT organizations. Staff members are critical of their managers for not being more proactive in providing developmental opportunities and frequently rank development as one of their top concerns in annual employee surveys. Yet the majority of staff members are reluctant—to the point of being fearful—of actually accepting a developmental assignment when presented with the opportunity.

No one turns down a developmental assignment if a promotion is involved. Individuals are happy to move to different parts of the organization, take on new functional responsibilities, work with a different team, and report to a new boss if they are receiving more money and a new title to do so. However, convincing individuals to take on lateral opportunities where no additional money or titles are involved can be like pulling teeth!

Individuals presented with lateral opportunities invariably want assurances that they can go back to their current positions if things don't work out as planned. They try to negotiate pay increases or promotions at some future date as a precondition for accepting a lateral assignment. In effect, they seek a risk-free developmental experience with guaranteed rewards.

All too often, managers actually lay the groundwork for such discussions by presenting the lateral opportunity as a hardship assignment that they would like an individual to accept "for the good of the company." The opportunity is presented as a *loyalty test* instead of a true developmental experience. Discussions of employee preconditions would be far fewer and much shorter if managers were more explicit about the skill or performance deficiencies that the lateral assignment was designed to address. It's hard to argue for no-fault escape clauses and guaranteed rewards when you're being told that there are concerns about the scope or scalability of your existing skills, or the need to develop new competencies to ensure a meaningful role in the company in the future. Good people managers can frame these discussions in constructive, nonthreatening terms but still get the point across that the risks associated with declining a lateral opportunity are far greater than the risks involved in accepting it!

Building a Talent Pipeline

Hiring opportunities rarely occur in a planned, premeditated fashion. In the real world, they tend to occur with little warning as the result of attrition, restructuring, merger and acquisition events, new business initiatives, or operational crises. Hiring opportunities can also be ephemeral. Approved job requisitions have a nasty habit of disappearing altogether if they can't be filled in a relatively short period of time.

Tactical hiring in response to transient opportunities can actually be counterproductive. It may simply propagate the existing skill mix of the team without adding any new capabilities. It may maintain or expand staffing in areas that will wane in importance over the next few years. It may result in the addition of individuals who have critical technical knowledge but lack the business experience, collaboration skills, or personal maturity to be truly effective. In short, tactical hiring may resolve short-term issues in a haphazard fashion without addressing any of the organization's strategic talent needs. In the worst case, tactical hiring may create or escalate a series of longer-term talent issues that offset any short-term benefits.

Strategic staffing plans are needed to ensure that the organization obtains the maximum benefits from hiring opportunities when they occur. But strategic plans are of little use unless they are accompanied by a concrete list of candidates who could assume specific organizational roles. If talent is truly the primary factor determining the success of an IT organization, then every IT manager should constantly be on the lookout for individuals who can fill the most urgently needed roles within her team. In other words, managers need to build and maintain a talent pipeline.

Successful sales organizations are quite adept at filling vacancies on short notice. It's a survival skill they develop to meet their annual sales targets. Field sales representatives resign on a regular basis if they feel they don't have the right mix of skills, products, or customers to meet their assigned quotas. Such resignations create organizational gaps that must be plugged quickly to ensure that the sales team achieves its collective targets. Seasoned sales leaders maintain an extensive network of acquaintances, associates, and former colleagues who can potentially be recruited to fill such gaps when they occur. These leaders constantly encourage their regional sales managers and area directors to identify individuals who could fill key roles if struggling team members suddenly quit. Successful sales managers maintain a constant pipeline of prospective job candidates and continually upgrade the talent on their teams.

IT managers need to be similarly proactive in developing a pipeline of prospective talent they can tap on short notice when hiring opportunities present themselves. A variety of mechanisms are available to build and nurture a talent pipeline. Seasoned managers fill their pipelines by stealing talent, developing talent, prospecting for talent, and attracting talent. Best results are achieved when all four of these sourcing mechanisms are pursued in parallel.

Stealing Talent

The most obvious sources of talent available to any manager are the teams he has managed in the past. Individuals who possessed the skills, aptitude, and maturity needed to succeed in the manager's former organization are highly likely to succeed in his new group as well. Some managers are unduly concerned about the consequences of recruiting former colleagues. They fear their new team will assume that key roles are being filled on the basis of past friendships instead of proven accomplishments. They want to avoid the perception that they're relying on an "old boys network" or "personal mafia" to be successful in their new roles. In fact, quite the opposite is likely true. Managers being recruited from other organizations are frequently expected to bring proven talent along with them, perhaps not immediately, but over time. This is especially true for individuals recruited into more senior roles. The people who hired you expect you to jump-start your new organization by seeding it with proven talent you've discovered in the past.

Managers are also fearful of undermining team morale by recruiting former associates and placing them in prominent positions. Team members may assume that the new manager has a bias against the capabilities of his inherited staff and conclude that their advancement opportunities are limited. Again, this concern is misplaced if the individuals being added to the organization possess clearly superior skills and leadership capabilities. IT staff members crave personal development opportunities. When they realize they can personally benefit from working with one of the manager's former colleagues, their fears and resentments will dissipate rapidly.

Finally, managers recruited from outside an organization should have very selfish reasons for recruiting proven talent from past companies, namely that they want to be successful themselves! Proven performers who bring skills and experience that directly contribute to the new leader's agenda are invaluable in delivering short-term results that can justify longer-term strategic initiatives.

Seeding New Skills

When managers need to introduce wholly new skills into their organizations they typically employ the services of external consultants to retrain existing staff members. This is especially true—in fact, it's a necessity—in organizations operating under strict head count restrictions. Experience has shown that retraining is a risky and unpredictable adventure. It always seems to be harder, take longer, and turn out to be less successful than everyone originally anticipated.

Retraining initiatives can fail for a variety of reasons. Staff members may become overly dependent on the consultants delivering the training and be lost when they depart. The training may provide a general framework for new skills or work practices but detailed specification of workflows, procedures, artifacts, etc., may still be left to the imagination of the existing staff, none of whom has prior experience with the skills or practices being deployed. Teams may be forced to implement new capabilities largely on their own due to funding limitations that restrict the use of consultants. Self-managed training programs frequently suffer from multiple false starts, excessive iterations, and one-of-a-kind results. Finally, existing staff members may actually resist retraining—either overtly or covertly—and attempt to sabotage such programs through a series of passive-aggressive behaviors.

Retraining campaigns usually produce mixed results. A small percentage of the existing staff "get it." They embrace the need for the new skills, they view the training as a personal development opportunity, and they become fully proficient in the new skills or work practices. An equally small percentage fail to develop an acceptable level of proficiency due to a lack of personal motivation or ability. Remaining staff members fall somewhere in between. They are proficient enough to get by, but you would never hire candidates with their skill level to fill job openings on the retrained team (you'd want someone better!).

The speed and success of reskilling initiatives are immeasurably improved when proven practitioners are added to the existing team on a permanent basis. Their previous experience can pay major dividends in specifying procedural work details that are both practical and effective, avoiding mistakes they've observed elsewhere, mentoring colleagues who need extra assistance, and maintaining momentum after the consultants depart. "There's no substitute for experience," as they say, and that's categorically true in introducing new skills or work practices into an existing team. While it's theoretically possible to retrain teams solely with consulting assistance, the likelihood of success and time to market of new capabilities will be significantly improved if "new blood" with proven expertise is added to the team.

Developing Talent

The second most logical source of talent is the manager's current team. Conventional approaches to talent development include formal instruction, on-the-job training, special assignments, and job rotation. Internal development is frequently incremental in nature and is intentionally designed to extend or complement an individual's existing capabilities. A more radical approach to talent development is to assign individuals to tasks or activities that are wholly outside the scope of their formal training or current responsibilities. For example, ask a technical architect within the enterprise architecture group to manage internal cloud operations for the product development team for the next ninety days. Or ask the leader of the ERP support team to lead a data center consolidation project. Cross-training individuals in areas outside their conventional comfort zones provides much more insight into their true growth potential. It can expand their future advancement opportunities and improve cross-disciplinary teamwork throughout the organization as well.

Many companies employ "high-potential" (HiPo) programs to provide emerging leaders with targeted developmental opportunities. These programs rarely succeed in expanding the talent pool. They fail to identify latent talent within the organization because most HiPo candidates are already well known to management. They frequently fail to deliver meaningful developmental experiences because they are overtaken by other events that distract management attention or place conflicting demands on the HiPos' time. In the final analysis, they can actually be counterproductive because they concentrate management attention on a very limited number of senior individuals at the expense of providing developmental opportunities for more junior staff members who would likely benefit from such experiences.

If your company conducts an annual HiPo planning exercise, you might challenge your team to develop a list of second-tier candidates who might qualify for the formal HiPo program in succeeding years. Providing prospective candidates with developmental opportunities will expand the size and diversity of the HiPo talent pool in subsequent years and likely improve retention rates for key individuals as well. The dedication and enthusiasm created by targeted developmental opportunities for junior staff members can truly be amazing.

Prospecting for Talent

Neighboring companies in your city or regional area are prime talent sources. It's immaterial whether such companies have business models or customers similar to yours. They still possess individuals with relevant technical knowledge and real-world business experience.

Vendors are prime sources of information about talent in other companies. They devote considerable effort to identifying technical leaders who can champion the use of their products. Over time, they develop considerable insight into the top performers within different organizations and are generally willing to share such insight, especially if it can advance their sales efforts. Consulting firms are also valuable prospecting resources because they frequently interact with the leading technologists and change agents within their client companies over the course of a typical engagement.

Local universities can be valuable talent sources as well. Intern and co-op programs provide an excellent means of screening college students and selectively hiring those that exhibit superior learning aptitudes, strong work ethics, and exceptional collaboration skills.

Attracting Talent

IT organizations establish reputations within their local communities that can help or hinder their recruiting efforts. Individual organizations may be stereotyped as being "very demanding" or "highly innovative" or "very political." Participation in local and regional industry events and a willingness to host such events can raise the visibility of an IT organization and significantly improve its external reputation. If an IT organization is reputed to be innovative, respectful of its employees' work–life balance, and well managed, it will attract unsolicited interest from a wide variety of employees at neighboring companies. Successful IT leaders develop a standard "stump speech" describing the business challenges, technical initiatives, and work culture within their organizations. They use it whenever possible to enhance the reputation of their team and stimulate interest among prospective job candidates.

Carpere Occasionem—Seize the Opportunity

Managers assuming new roles have unique opportunities to churn their talent pools and uncover some of the latent talent within their organizations. New managers are implicitly (and sometimes explicitly) expected to shake things up and alter existing team structures and work assignments. This opportunity should be seized and acted upon while such expectations are prevalent across the organization. Managers who procrastinate and opt for analysis over action will soon find themselves ensnared in the same web of individual preferences, prejudices, and promotion expectations that has paralyzed internal talent movements in the past. Team members will become increasingly reluctant to support changes in team structure or work assignments as the initial period of high-change expectations wanes.

There's never a perfect time to reorganize an IT group. Any

reorganization will inevitably create some form of collateral emotional damage that management needs to address. Organizational changes don't become any easier to plan or implement when they're deferred beyond the initial honeymoon period that accompanies the arrival of a newly appointed leader. Teams expect organizational changes to occur when new leaders are appointed. They should not be disappointed!

Chapter 4

Playing Nicely with the Vendors

Cloud computing has had a revolutionary impact on the internal operations of many, if not most, IT organizations. It has had an equally profound impact on the relationships IT organizations have with their suppliers.

Before cloud computing, IT shops functioned as general contractors responsible for the detailed design, physical construction, and long-term maintenance of the systems that delivered essential IT services to an enterprise. Vendors supplied the raw materials for these construction efforts in the form of data center hardware and telecom circuits. Business applications were either developed internally or licensed from commercial vendors. IT shops hosted the majority of their business applications and supported a diverse array of server and storage technologies in their data centers.

This was the "caveman era" of system construction, in which IT professionals ventured out of their organizations, surveyed the capabilities of various vendor products, selected individual technology components, and then dragged the selected products back into their caves to be assembled into systems that could support specific business processes. The buyers of IT products and services occupied a position of unassailable power in their relationships with most vendors because they could easily substitute component technologies from one vendor with roughly equivalent capabilities from another. Many IT shops intentionally maintained two-vendor buying strategies for critical technologies to ensure an ongoing cost competition among their suppliers. At first glance a two-vendor strategy would appear to be highly desirable from the buyers' perspective but it also resulted in significant hidden costs related to the integration and maintenance of duplicative technologies.

The caveman era of system construction has passed. Few shops engage in buy-versus-build debates anymore. The presumption is that new capabilities will be largely procured as cloud-based services, pre-integrated stacks of data center hardware, or managed services. SaaS applications have become ubiquitous and have replaced a wide variety of homegrown applications and licensed software packages. Hardware vendors are touting the benefits of converged infrastructure appliances in which server/storage/network devices arrive at the data center as pre-integrated modules or pods, requiring no assembly. Some of these pre-integrated hardware stacks provide the vendors with continuous telemetry regarding their health and performance. Vendors can take preemptive measures to address potential hardware issues based on this telemetry, significantly reducing the skills the IT organization needs to detect, diagnose, and rectify hardware-related problems. Alternatively, the organization can elect to move its data center operations into a public cloud and avoid hardware operational concerns altogether. Finally, managed service vendors supply hard-to-find skills in such areas as network operations or information security management, again reducing the IT organization's need to maintain such skills in-house.

The shopping experience of the IT buyer has changed significantly in this new world. If the shopping experience in the caveman era resembled a visit to a local grocery store to procure the ingredients required for a home-cooked meal, the current experience is much more akin to visiting the ready-to-go counter at a local Whole Foods store and purchasing precooked items that can be assembled into a meal. The buyers still possess the upper hand in this buy–sell relationship because they hold the money sought by the sellers. However, the breadth of their selections has changed and their ability to customize their "meal" has also become more limited.

In the earlier era of buy–sell transactions, the relationship between IT leaders and vendors was frequently adversarial. IT leaders were expected to extract every ounce of advantage from their dealings with vendors. They were rewarded for contesting a vendor's capabilities, pricing, and contract terms to the maximum degree possible. Vendors contributed to these adversarial behaviors by making inflated claims regarding the capabilities of their products or making unrealistic demands during pricing negotiations. The adversarial relationships that were fostered and encouraged in the past are largely anachronistic in the current IT marketplace and can sometimes be counterproductive.

IT organizations no longer have the staffing levels or skills required to manage an ever-expanding portfolio of component technologies. Even if they had the requisite staff and skills, their internal customers no longer have the patience to suffer through the construction process described above when such capabilities can be acquired on a pre-made basis from cloud or managed service vendors. The prepackaged on-demand capabilities of cloud vendors can literally be implemented in a matter of days or weeks, while the construction approach to creating comparable capabilities requires months or quarters.

The job of the IT leader in today's environment is to aggregate and integrate services offered by competing vendors instead of buying component technologies that must be assembled and maintained in-house. This is not a particularly new or profound insight, but in adjusting to this new paradigm IT leaders need to develop a new mindset in the way they approach vendor-selection decisions and the relationships they maintain with their vendors. IT leaders still hold the money the vendors are ultimately seeking, but in today's world the IT leader will be much more reliant on the vendor's product plans and operational competence, because the IT organization has surrendered physical control of its applications and infrastructure in exchange for increased agility and potentially lower costs.

Vendors have realized they can benefit significantly by leading rather than resisting this process of service aggregation and integration. In a marked departure from past practices, many have exposed the programming interfaces associated with their products to other vendors offering complementary capabilities. Salesforce.com is a leading proponent of this strategy. More than two thousand software and data service firms have interfaced their commercial offerings to Salesforce and joined the AppExchange, Salesforce's business applications store. AppExchange companies offer a wide array of customer-facing capabilities in the areas of sales, marketing, customer support, and business intelligence. Salesforce customers have downloaded AppExchange products more than three million times since its inception in 2006.

In effect, Salesforce has established an ecosystem of vendors, each offering different but interrelated capabilities. Other vendors are pursuing similar strategies, trying to turn suites of existing products into platforms that vendors with complementary capabilities can access and build upon. In today's world, IT leaders need to selectively knit together the capabilities of different vendor ecosystems in ways that satisfy their business needs.

IT leaders need to approach this new type of marketplace in a very different way than they have in the past. In many instances, buyers are no longer purchasing a single product or service. Instead, they are aligning their organizations with various supplier confederations. Each confederation or ecosystem offers a wide range of capabilities that may prove useful in the future even if some or most of those capabilities are irrelevant to a company's immediate needs. Shopping in this marketplace is more a matter of forming alliances with industry-leading platforms than of procuring specific products or services. Platforms offering the widest range of functionality, the deepest degrees of integration and the most comprehensive security safeguards will provide the greatest long-term benefits in responding to emerging business needs and opportunities.

While the vendors are busy assembling their ecosystems, IT

organizations must do likewise. Every IT shop has to selectively knit together the platform capabilities of its major suppliers and surgically implement the cross-platform functionality that is uniquely suited to support its company's business processes. In today's marketplace, IT leaders need to build an ecosystem of ecosystems that is customized and optimized for the distinctive needs of their business.

In the caveman construction era, IT organizations were highly reliant on construction skills such as software coding and testing, hardware installation and integration, and change and release management. In the emerging era of ecosystem integration, these technical skills will be superseded by the need to manage infrastructure utilization, end-user experience, data integrity, and security safeguards. These are the new core competencies of the ecosystem era, and they will become increasingly important in evaluating vendor capabilities in the future.

The advent of cloud computing and the ubiquitous buildout of vendor platforms have fundamentally altered the balance of power between IT buyers and sellers. Buyers still control the investment dollars that are the ultimate source of power in the buy–sell relationship. But platform vendors offering extended software and infrastructure capabilities are increasingly dominating the marketplace and limiting the buying options available to large enterprise buyers.

Selecting the Right Vendors for Your Ecosystem

The revolution occurring in the vendor marketplace is having a significant ripple effect on the procedures IT shops employ to evaluate vendor offerings. The conventional evaluation process employed in the past was formal, time consuming, and ultimately quite frustrating for the buyer and the seller. IT shops would customarily construct a "long list" of prospective vendors based upon the prognostications of various industry research groups and the capabilities of incumbent vendors currently supplying products or services to the organization. Long-list candidates would typically be given an opportunity to present an introductory briefing or demonstration summarizing their product's capabilities. A short list of three to six candidates was culled from this exercise for further analysis.

Functional requirements for new capabilities were commonly documented by business systems analysts (BSAs), sometimes in exhausting detail. Nonfunctional requirements regarding adherence to architectural standards, product supportability, upgrade frequency, etc., were routinely incorporated in such documents as well, generally making them quite lengthy and complex.

Short-list candidates were asked to score the capabilities of their products relative to the selection criteria enumerated in the requirements documents. The two to three candidates with the highest ratings were subsequently invited to conduct proof-of-concept (POC) exercises at the customer's site to validate the capabilities of their product. The winners of the POC competition were subsequently asked to identify reference customers who could be contacted to further validate the vendor's claims. Many reference calls were largely pro forma in nature because the existing customers had little to gain by sharing critical information about the vendor's capabilities or performance. Consequently, most IT organizations placed far more reliance on the first-hand experience they obtained through on-site POC evaluations than in the feedback they received from reference customers.

This type of process was flawed in several respects. Up to six months could easily be required to select a preferred product before any contractual negotiations had taken place and well before any substantive work was being performed to derive business benefits from the product. The requirements scoring process could also be maddening. Business users from different regions or operating divisions might rate products very differently, leaving IT in a quandary as to whose perceptions were most accurate or most politically important. After averaging the scores of multiple evaluators, the summary ratings for the finalist candidates would frequently differ by less than 10 percent. Under these circumstances, the final selection decision would be based on pricing instead of functionality (an outcome that most of the BSAs had likely predicted at the outset of the evaluation!).

The evaluation of cloud-based services and extended vendor platforms can be performed in a much more agile and accelerated fashion. Formal requirement documents are largely a thing of the past. Vendors can provide sandbox testing environments that are fully functional versions of their product or service for the exclusive use of the prospective customer. These environments can be configured, loaded with real-world customer data, and tested immediately, with minimal planning and preparation. Other services can be employed on a trial basis, potentially free of charge.

In a general sense, sandbox exercises or trial subscriptions serve the same overall purpose as the former POC activities. Both are designed to determine "goodness of fit" between a customer's needs and a vendor's offering. But upon closer inspection, the rules of the game have changed quite fundamentally. In the past, vendors were asked to score their capabilities against a customer's business requirements. In today's world, the customers are asked to evaluate the adaptability of their business processes to the vendor's capabilities. This distinction is subtle but it reflects the profound difference between building specialized systems that satisfy highly customized requirements and subscribing to standardized offerings that are architecturally and operationally controlled by the vendors.

Immediate access to fully functional vendor offerings that can be configured to suit the needs of a prospective customer can significantly compress the vendor evaluation, selection, and implementation timeline, thereby accelerating the time-to-business benefits. Business representatives can play a much more substantive role in this compressed process, allowing the IT organization to leverage their enthusiasm and support in obtaining the funds needed to purchase the product or service.

Selection criteria are also somewhat different than they were in the past. The road map the vendor has established to extend the capabilities of its product becomes much more critical because it's no longer easy nor necessarily desirable to customize the product in response to the unique needs of individual customers. Operational competencies related to reliability, response times, and information security may be of equal or greater importance than the functional capabilities of the vendor offering. As platforms proliferate, the partnerships the vendor has formed with companies offering complementary capabilities become an increasingly important factor in the final selection decision as well. Even if your business has no immediate needs for specific platform capabilities at the present time, the vendor possessing the broadest ecosystem of complementary capabilities offers the greatest long-term business benefits, all other factors being equal.

Social collaboration tools have largely displaced formal reference calls as a means of obtaining information from a vendor's current customers. Blogs, chat rooms, and online user group meetings can provide a wealth of information about the difficulties others have experienced in implementing a specific product. Informal interactions with current customers can provide insight into the ways in which the vendor's capabilities have been adapted to support business processes similar to yours. Collaboration tools such as LinkedIn provide ready access to colleagues at other companies that are known to be using the product you are considering. As a professional courtesy, many CIOs and VPs will provide access to the members of their teams who are most familiar with the product under evaluation when contacted by their peers at other companies. All of these communication channels lie outside the conventional reference call procedure described above and should be exploited to the maximum extent possible before making a final decision.

It's important to note that the formal selection procedures employed in the past may still be appropriate in certain situations. The procurement activities of government agencies and public utilities are highly scrutinized and may require meticulous documentation of the criteria and procedures employed in vendor evaluation, as well as the scoring results that justified final selection decisions. Large enterprises with competing internal constituencies may also employ more formal and scripted evaluation procedures to adjudicate the divergent interests of different stakeholder groups.

Relationship Buying Versus Relationship Selling

Product capabilities and product pricing play a critical role in any vendor selection process but final procurement decisions frequently hinge on the personal relationships that a vendor's account manager establishes with individual IT leaders. Setting aside all the effort devoted to product evaluation and contract negotiation, a simple truth remains: people prefer to buy stuff from people they like and trust. It's invariably harder to sell products or services to someone who dislikes you or distrusts your company. An account manager will likely close a sale if his product has clearly superior capabilities and competitive pricing or if it has adequate capabilities and compelling pricing. But the sales process leading to the "win" will likely be more protracted and much more painful if he is disliked or distrusted.

IT vendors are acutely aware of the importance of establishing amicable, respectful, and trusting relationships with their customers. They devote extensive portions of their sales training programs to the art of listening effectively, understanding their customers' business strategies, cultivating social relationships with key decision makers, and describing the utility of their products in business terms instead of technical jargon. Sales trainees conduct role-playing exercises to practice conversations that convey intense interest in a customer's business priorities or sow seeds of doubt regarding their competitors' capabilities. The goal of these training programs is to equip account managers with the skills they need to establish authentic, trustworthy, and strategic relationships with prospective buyers. Few IT leaders who have not had direct work experience in a vendor organization can appreciate the sophistication of these training programs or the scientific manner in which sales campaigns in major accounts are actually conducted.

IT leaders need some complementary training to fully understand the selling strategies and priorities of their vendors' account managers. While some account managers are sincerely motivated by a desire to solve a tactical problem or support a strategic initiative within a targeted account, their suggestions regarding the scope, size, and timing of any future procurements need to be interpreted through the lens of their incentive programs. Incentive programs for large enterprise IT vendors can be very complex. At any given point in time, premiums may be placed on selling into a new account, selling a newly released product, selling an existing product in conjunction with a partner's product, selling in a new geography, selling a managed service instead of a product, selling professional services to assist in implementing a specific product, etc. In a perfect world, an account manager understands your needs and has customized his sales proposal to ensure that you get the maximum bang for the buck from any future purchase. In the real world, an account manager's sales pitch will be influenced, in whole or in part, by the combination of products and services that provide her with the greatest financial rewards. That may sound harsh or overly judgmental but it's an inescapable truth!

IT managers need advanced training in the incentive plans employed by their vendors so they can make more informed decisions about the nature, size, and timing of different procurement scenarios. Trust is a two-way street! If the buyer can't be trusted with information concerning sales incentives, why should the seller be trusted with information regarding the buyer's budget and business priorities? IT managers need to become more proficient in relationship buying to offset the training that their account managers are receiving in relationship selling.

Continuing Your Education

The vast majority of current IT leaders achieved early success in their careers on the basis of their technical skills. Many harbor the mistaken belief that they have maintained their technical prowess as their careers evolved. In fact, quite the opposite has occurred. Software engineering skills that are considered to be industry standard today were unknown ten years ago. Specialized hardware devices of the past are being deconstructed into software applications that can run on commodity hardware, leading to the emergence of software-defined networking and storage technologies that were unknown five years ago. Most of the technical knowledge that fueled the initial success of a current IT leader is now likely to be erroneous or irrelevant!

Vendors are a valuable source of information about current trends within the IT industry. Most would be thrilled to host a visit by a CIO or VP or senior director to share their views about the challenges of their customers, the failings of their competitors, and their vision for the future within their particular area of expertise. Vendor account managers and their regional sales directors would be equally anxious to establish networking opportunities for IT leaders with their peers at other companies. These relationships can be mined not just for information on a product or service currently under evaluation but for the discussion of a much broader range of topics as well.

Leaders who seek to further their technical education through interactions with vendors should structure such discussions carefully. Account managers routinely receive training on the capabilities of the products they are selling. But they rarely have any firsthand knowledge about implementing or using such products themselves. Most account managers would be the first to admit that they are not technical experts and would likely urge an IT leader to spend time with other, more technical members of their organization. A vendor's presales technical consultants have far more insight into the capabilities of their products but are still primarily motivated to achieve their assigned sales targets. Consequently, they will be reluctant to discuss a product's functional limitations or chronic operational issues with a prospective customer.

Visits to the vendor's headquarters or product development center are likely to be far more educational. In arranging these types of visits, IT leaders should specifically request interactions with product managers or architects, or with engagement managers from the vendor's professional services team. Individuals in these roles have much more practical experience regarding the capabilities and limitations of the vendor's offering, and are much more likely to share their insights because they are not incented to achieve individual sales targets. If visitors fail to specify the types of individuals they would like to meet during their visits, they will end up receiving standard presentations prepared by the vendor's technical marketing team. These canned presentations will be delivered by professional briefers whose personal familiarity with the vendor's offering is frequently limited or dated.

IT management is sometimes characterized as a form of intellectual strip mining, in which an individual's current employer extracts every last ounce of knowledge and experience the leader has to offer while providing very little knowledge or training in return. Vendors provide a unique vehicle to redress this imbalance. Their willingness to discuss and debate industry trends and expose IT leaders to peers dealing with similar issues are unique educational opportunities not readily accessible to most IT staff members. Wise IT leaders will exploit such opportunities to the maximum extent possible.

Vendors As Anthropologists

Anthropology is the study of human behavior. Anthropologists conduct fieldwork to observe how people behave as individuals and in groups, how they communicate and socialize with one another, and how they adapt to change. Vendor account managers must develop behavioral research skills if they hope to generate new sales, either in existing accounts or new ones. The most successful account managers would probably qualify as full-fledged anthropologists, although it might never occur to them to characterize themselves as research scientists!

Account managers are trained to identify "champions," "decision makers," and "influencers" within every prospective account. A champion is typically a technical expert who is willing to evangelize the capabilities of the vendor's product among his peers and managers. A decision maker is the individual who has ultimate spending authority for the funding that will be needed to procure the vendor's product. Influencers are trusted compatriots of the decision maker and serve as his key advisors. The opinions and recommendations of the influencers will ultimately determine the outcome of the sales process.

Account managers also invest considerable time and energy in analyzing the decision-making processes within a prospective customer organization. In companies with strong biases toward consensual decision making, the account manager may be forced to orchestrate the buying decision herself, to ensure that relevant information regarding the purchase of her product is fully socialized across all relevant stakeholders within the IT, finance, and procurement teams.

Account managers learn a lot about an IT organization as they perform the due diligence required to sell into a new account or expand sales within an existing account. They identify the true thought leaders within the customer organization and determine their technical biases and prejudices. They discover personal animosities among staff members and managers that may impede or obstruct a potential buying decision. They may also uncover chronic issues regarding the perceived competence or credibility of the IT organization that further complicate the purchase approval process.

Anthropological insights are developed through prolonged exposure to human behaviors within the customer organization as well as through the ability to compare the cultural practices of one IT organization with those of another. Some account managers lack the intelligence or experience to discern behavioral differences among various IT organizations. Others are simply too new to the accounts they are managing and don't have the empirical data needed to detect recurring patterns of behavior. However, seasoned account managers who have worked with individual customers for multiple years possess a wealth of knowledge about the dysfunctional behaviors and flawed processes that exist within the customer's organization. Their insights can be extremely valuable to any IT manager or leader.

Anyone who believes that account managers fail to develop such insights should be given an opportunity to participate in the "prep call" (short for preparation call) that precedes a sales team's visit to a customer organization. The participants on the call typically include the account manager, one or more presales technical specialists, and perhaps additional sales managers, professional services consultants, or even a member of the vendor's product development team. During the prep call the account manager will provide a succinct and sometimes lethal summary of the knowledge, intelligence, and effectiveness of each customer representative participating in the on-site meeting. The account manager will provide more feedback on the competence and performance of these individuals than they have probably received during their past three performance reviews!

As a rule, account managers rarely share their anthropological insights with IT leaders, for the obvious reason that they are reluctant to jeopardize any of the interpersonal relationships they've developed through months of on-site fieldwork. Enlightened IT leaders need to establish some type of "safety net" or "demilitarized zone" in which savvy account managers can freely share their perceptions about the strengths and weaknesses of the leader's organization without fear of reprisal.

Leaders who have dealt fairly with major vendors on a consistent basis throughout their careers will discover that they can establish political safety nets for such discussions with relative ease. Leaders who have historically treated vendors with condescension or contention will find it much more difficult to do so. (Here's a tip: if you established a collaborative working relationship with an account manager at a previous employer, ask that individual to inform their sales colleague at your current company that you are someone who can be trusted. If you had an effective working relationship with the account manager at your previous company, you will likely be able to accelerate the development of a similar relationship with his counterpart at your current company.)

IT organizations develop well-defined personas within the vendor community. Some organizations are labeled as being "highly political" or "old-fashioned" or "unable to make decisions." Individuals within IT shops also develop reputations as being "innovative" or "dictatorial" or "widely disliked." These perceptions may be pervasive outside your organization but not readily appreciated internally. This is very valuable feedback for an IT leader trying to establish a high-performance team. The same information is no doubt discoverable through personal observation and on-the-job experience, but it can be obtained much more quickly and directly by leveraging the insights of the vendors servicing your organization. This type of information is especially useful for a newly appointed manager. In many instances an incoming manager can learn more about his organization in a sixty-minute conversation with an insightful account manager than he can in six months of personal experience!

Who Is My Judy?

Several years ago, I was teaching a seminar on vendor management practices with another CIO. During my presentation I talked about the general responsibilities of sales account managers and specifically described the role they play in preparing for a sales team visit to a prospective customer. Preparation calls are routinely scheduled before such visits to ensure that all sales team members understand the roles and responsibilities of the individuals they will meet. In addition, account managers are expected to share their insights regarding the technical competence, personal biases, business reputations, and political influence of the individuals participating in the meeting. To illustrate the conversation that typically takes place during a prep call I created the following fictional dialogue.

> *Account manager:* When we get in the room, Bob will be sitting at the head of the table. He's the ultimate decision maker but he won't say much. He's not technical enough to understand what our product can actually do, so he'll rely on the opinion of others. John is our champion but everyone knows he's fallen in love with our product. They think he's completely lost his objectivity, so his comments will mostly be ignored by everyone else in the room. Tom still believes in custom development. He'll argue that their current web application can already do 60 percent of what our product offers, and if he was simply given three contractors for six months he could easily reproduce the capabilities of our product. Everyone knows that Tom likes to build things and he would always rather build than buy, so no one will take him seriously but he will talk

a lot. Judy is really smart and really likes the capabilities of our low-cost competitor but she works remotely and her peers don't like working with her. They think she hogs all the credit when things go right and disappears when things go wrong. Her opinion won't count for much during the group discussion. Steve will challenge everyone as to why they need to buy our product now, but everyone knows he's retiring next year so they don't really care what he thinks. Finally, Jane will sit somewhere in the middle of the table and she won't ask any questions but she's the ultimate influencer in the buying decision. She and Bob went to the same local college and their boys play on the same baseball team. Bob will ultimately go with Jane's recommendation but she won't tip her hand at this meeting.

Through sheer coincidence, the other CIO who was co-teaching this seminar was a sales target of my current employer at the time. I had personally participated in a recent sales visit to his organization. When I sat down next to him at the conclusion of my presentation, he leaned over and whispered, "Who is my Judy?"

Chapter 5

What Gets Measured Gets Managed

Everyone agrees that metrics play a critical role in managing the performance of an IT organization, but few management teams make effective use of them. Most IT shops are drowning in metrics. They employ a wide variety of tools and systems that generate a continuous stream of metrics. Their support vendors report performance relative to the service level metrics specified in their contracts. Still other metrics are imposed on IT by corporate finance or HR or the internal audit team. It's not all that surprising that metrics are largely ignored by IT groups because there are simply so many of them!

Metrics serve two primary purposes. First, they establish objective reality. In a large, dispersed IT organization it can be quite difficult to accurately gauge overall performance. Key indicators may be measured in different ways in different operating locations or may not be measured at all in others. Anecdotal information may be readily available, but it can be extremely difficult to verify, calibrate, or interpret. Subjective interpretations of inconsistent data and random anecdotes can easily lead to erroneous conclusions regarding organizational performance.

The second primary purpose of metrics is to modify the behavior of individuals and organizations. Metrics provide a means of maintaining organizational focus on strategic goals and objectives. They can also be used in a narrower context to fix tactical problems and correct operational deficiencies. Human behavior is a hard thing to predict. Although metrics can inspire and promote desired behaviors, they may inadvertently trigger unanticipated and undesirable behaviors as well.

IT organizations have an instinctive affinity for metrics. Most managers and staff members received academic training in math, science, or engineering early in their careers. They possess sophisticated data collection and analysis skills. They instinctively rely on quantitative information to develop plans and make decisions. To most members of the IT team, metrics represent a natural and logical way of monitoring and managing performance. Consequently, they surround themselves with metrics that serve a wide variety of purposes, ranging from daily operational hygiene to tactical process improvement to strategic organizational change.

Any management team seeking to develop a metrics scorecard needs to identify performance measures that satisfy four critical criteria. Meaningful metrics must be definable, measurable, comprehensible, and sustainable, as discussed below.

- *Definable:* Metrics must be defined in a precise fashion that can be applied consistently across the entire organization. Some metrics may need to be defined on a situational basis to be truly meaningful.

- *Measurable:* Although it's easy to imagine hypothetical metrics that would be excellent barometers of organizational performance, they may require inordinate effort to measure and thus be impractical.

- *Comprehensible:* If metrics are being established to influence staff behavior, they need to make sense to staff members. If they are too narrow or specialized, or if too few staff members have any way of influencing a specific metric, then it's unlikely to have a significant behavioral impact. The best metrics are intuitively comprehensible to the broadest possible cross section of staff members.

• *Sustainable:* Most IT shops have experienced a series of metrics fads. If a management team establishes a metrics program, it must commit to maintaining the program for a significant period of time. Otherwise, the staff will pay little attention to the current fad and metrics will have no appreciable impact on organizational performance.

Although these criteria appear simple and straightforward in principle, they can be devilishly hard to satisfy in practice. A classic example of a seemingly simple metric is system downtime. All IT organizations are dedicated to ensuring their critical business systems are available to users 24×7. System downtime is bad, and should be minimized at all costs. Consequently, downtime is one of the most common metrics incorporated into performance scorecards.

What is the proper definition of system downtime? If a system was taken offline for planned maintenance, was it down? If problems occurred during the maintenance window and the window was extended, was the system down if no users attempted to log on during the extension period? If there was a network outage in a specific part of the world that made the system inaccessible to a limited number of local users, was the system down? If the database supporting the system was not being updated on its normal schedule but the system was still responding to user queries with somewhat dated information, was it down? The list of special circumstances that can impact the measurement of even a single metric is extensive. When metrics directly reflect the performance of specific individuals or teams (which is desirable), there will be countless special circumstances that staff members will want to incorporate into metric calculations.

Even in instances where measurement procedures are clearly defined, managers are frequently surprised and somewhat overwhelmed by the amount of work involved in compiling, analyzing, and interpreting metrics data. Metrics aren't "free." They don't automatically appear at the end of a week, a month, or a quarter at the mere touch of a button. Even when data collection procedures have become well established, analysis is still required to ensure that trends and variances are being interpreted correctly. When a metrics initiative is in its formative stages, staff members will frequently volunteer to assist in the selection, definition, and initial measurement of key performance indicators. Once the initiative has been institutionalized, the initial volunteers complain that metrics administration is not part of their regular jobs and that management needs to hire someone who can administer the program on an ongoing basis.

In many instances, metrics are changed too frequently. Managers lose interest in the metrics they championed three quarters ago and are preoccupied with a different set of concerns. Metrics obviously need to evolve and change over time to remain relevant. But if they are altered too frequently, the organization will learn to ignore them altogether.

Metrics are underutilized precisely because they are hard to define, hard to measure, hard to comprehend, and hard to sustain. Nevertheless, when chosen correctly, they remain powerful tools for motivating and focusing the efforts of diverse work teams. For better or worse, management teams launching performance improvement programs have a wide variety of potential metrics to choose from.

The Metrics Smorgasbord

Robert Kaplan and David Norton, two Harvard professors, popularized the concept of balanced scorecards roughly fifteen years ago. Balanced scorecards contain a collection of metrics grouped into four general categories: financial management, internal process efficiency, customer satisfaction, and organizational learning. These categories may or may not represent the challenges facing a specific IT shop, but they underscore the need to construct scorecards that address multiple dimensions of organizational performance. The most common dimensions of organizational performance are discussed below.

Financial Performance

Financial metrics are ubiquitous in most IT shops. Spending variances are monitored with maddening frequency and painful precision by the corporate finance team. Depreciation charges for past capital investments are tracked meticulously. Vendor billings are scrutinized for conformity with vendor contracts and customer expectations. In short, a tremendous amount of attention is customarily focused on financial metrics. IT managers need to seriously question whether additional emphasis is required to improve an organization's financial discipline.

Many financial metrics are lagging performance indicators, documenting financial conditions after they occur. Consequently, they're more useful in keeping spending problems from getting worse than in avoiding them altogether. IT teams would be better served if they focused on activities that perennially cause financial problems and build metrics around the management of those activities, rather than relying on financial metrics to help solve recurring financial issues. For example, individual shops may incur unanticipated expenses due to chronic delays on major projects, failure to dismiss contractors on schedule, or the uncontrolled proliferation of software licenses. If specific management issues create recurring financial problems, metrics programs should be used to promote behaviors that will resolve the root cause issues giving rise to the recurring problems.

Operational Performance

In many ways, operational metrics are the most appealing metrics for an IT management team to incorporate in a performance scorecard. The definition of such metrics and targeted levels of performance are largely within IT's control. A significant cross section of the organization can presumably influence or impact such metrics. Properly chosen, operational metrics can also serve as leading indicators of broader improvements in staff productivity, organizational effectiveness, and customer satisfaction. The principal downside of operational metrics is that they're typically ignored by executives and functional groups outside IT. Outsiders don't have the knowledge or insight to truly appreciate the significance of operational IT metrics.

Reading the Bible to a Cat

Many IT organizations employ relationship managers or service managers to coordinate the delivery of IT services to individual business teams. Service managers function as the principal points of contact for any and all IT concerns within their assigned teams, ranging from desktop support issues to system enhancement requests. I introduced service managers in a prior company and established quarterly service reviews (QSRs) with key business leaders to ensure that the leaders were fully aware of the support services they were receiving. The QSRs were designed to highlight major support issues and accomplishments during the past 90 days, obtain feedback on our performance, and discuss the business team's priorities for the next 90 to 180 days.

One of the initial QSRs was held with the leader of the order management team and his top lieutenants. The service manager assigned to the order management team gave a formal presentation at the QSR that meticulously documented a variety of team-specific metrics, including the downtime of their key support systems; the timing and duration of relevant maintenance windows; response times for trouble tickets submitted by their team members; system change requests implemented during the past 90 days; enhancements planned over the next quarter, etc. The leader of the order management function sat patiently through this presentation, then turned to one of his key lieutenants and asked, "Were we unable to process any orders during the last two weeks of the quarter due to an IT problem?" When the answer was no, he turned to us and said, "That's the only thing that I really care about...we really don't need to have these kind of reviews anymore." That's when I realized that, although he had sat through the entire presentation in rapt attention, he really had no interest in or understanding of the operational information we were presenting. It was like reading the Bible to a cat. The cat will stare at you the entire time and appear to be deeply contemplating every word you say, but it has absolutely no idea what you are talking about!

Customer Satisfaction

IT organizations generally have two sets of customers who employ very different criteria in assessing IT performance. The majority of employees interact with IT via the IT service desk. They submit their problems and requests to the desk and gauge performance in terms of the treatment they receive. Customer satisfaction levels are high when employee issues are resolved in a prompt, empathetic fashion. Satisfaction levels decline if the desk agents lack the necessary technical knowledge to resolve issues satisfactorily or fail to display an appropriate sense of respect and urgency in responding to employee concerns. The overall performance of the service desk is ultimately determined by the technical competence and interpersonal skills of the desk agents.

Business executives and senior managers constitute the second set of customers IT must serve. The criteria they employ to measure IT performance are quite different. They typically receive specialized support for their personal productivity needs and don't deal with the service desk. They are concerned primarily with IT's ability to support business initiatives and deliver new capabilities on time and on budget.

Given the polar differences in the perspectives of these two customer groups, accurate information regarding customer perceptions, customer satisfaction, and customer experience must be obtained in different ways. Service desks routinely send transactional surveys to their customers seeking feedback on the service they've received. Most customers ignore such requests. Response rates are typically less than 5 percent. Individuals who do respond generally fall into one of two camps. The majority gush with praise regarding the treatment they've received while the minority are severely dissatisfied and sometimes irate. When these extreme responses are averaged together and reported as a summary statistic, the desk's performance usually appears to be highly commendable. Desk satisfaction levels tend to be quite stable and rarely change significantly from month to month or quarter to quarter. Service desk satisfaction metrics should be treated cautiously because of the low survey response rates and the low variability in averaged ratings.

Some shops try to obtain more insightful feedback by having external consultants interview internal customers—both average employees and business executives. The use of consultants inevitably complicates such feedback because the consultants tend to employ their own biases and preconceived notions in filtering interviewee responses. In addition, the consultants frequently want to use the survey results to launch a more extensive consulting engagement to help "fix the problems" they allegedly discover.

In summary, although it's obviously desirable to incorporate some measure of customer satisfaction into an IT scorecard, it's extremely difficult to define metrics that are timely, easily measurable, and truly representative of customer perceptions. If the chronic causes of customer dissatisfaction are known or suspected, it's more productive to focus metrics on fixing the causes of such dissatisfaction rather than conducting surveys that produce ambiguous and sometimes misleading results.

Business Performance

Almost every major IT project is justified on the basis of business benefits. The business benefits resulting from IT investments are typically described in terms of revenue growth, cost reduction, employee productivity, and the retention of paying customers. Upgrades to existing systems produce similar benefits. Management consultants constantly urge IT leaders to develop systematic ways of measuring such benefits but few IT shops actually do so.

IT managers should never collect or report business metrics on behalf of business process owners or business leaders. Business metrics are notoriously difficult to measure. So many factors can impact the business outcome of an IT investment that it is difficult, if not impossible, to isolate IT's contribution to the outcome. Furthermore, IT managers lack the domain knowledge required to defend the analysis and interpretation of business metrics. They run the risk of appearing ignorant or naïve when engaging in such discussions. IT managers should be extremely wary of producing business metrics for business partners—this is ultimately the responsibility of the business leaders themselves, not IT.

Organizational Health

Companies employ a wide variety of metrics to gauge the morale and development of their employees. Some conduct engagement surveys that assess employee satisfaction with the nature of the work they are asked to perform, their relationships with supervisors and coworkers, the availability of training programs, advancement opportunities, etc. Others promote career development by monitoring the completion of performance reviews, per capita spending on training programs, merit pay participation rates, and promotion percentages. Attrition is another common barometer of organizational health, but it's difficult to establish a reasonable target—too many voluntary departures may be considered to be bad, but too few is bad too!

All organizations aspire to have high morale and are committed to the career development of their team members, but, once again, it's difficult to define and measure metrics that are meaningful to a broad cross section of stakeholders. Managers need to exercise extra caution in assessing organizational health through the use of globally averaged metrics, particularly in large, dispersed organizations. Global averages may camouflage significant morale or development issues within individual offices or work locations.

Security and Regulatory Integrity

Metrics employed to monitor compliance with industry or government regulations such as PCI, HIPAA, or SOX are well established and undoubtedly being tracked by both internal and external auditors. In most industries, IT doesn't need to invest additional effort in defining or tracking regulatory metrics.

Quite the opposite is true with respect to information security metrics. There are no widely accepted metrics regarding the integrity of information security practices. Many companies simply monitor trends in PC encryption, blocked viruses, time-to-quarantine infected servers, etc., because industry-standard benchmarks are not readily available. While it's critically important for information security teams to establish and track metrics, extreme caution should be exercised in promoting such metrics as broader performance indicators for the entire IT group. Most members of the IT organization will have very limited ability to influence security metrics. Furthermore, such metrics can easily raise more questions than they answer and can give outsiders a false sense of security or paranoia that is wholly unjustified.

Choosing the Right Metrics

By now it should be obvious that there is no one "right set" of standardized metrics that can be universally applied to all IT organizations. Management teams that embark on metrics initiatives need to pause and first determine what problems they are trying to solve. Are they trying to address internal operational or morale issues? Are they trying to enhance the effectiveness of the organization in the eyes of its customers? Are they trying to support new business strategies or initiatives? The answers to these questions should determine the performance dimensions employed in constructing a metrics dashboard.

A cardinal rule of any metrics initiative is "less is more." All too frequently, management teams fail to reach agreement about the metrics that are most meaningful to their organizations and simply incorporate all competing ideas in the initial program. A laundry list of performance metrics will inevitably overwhelm the staff and overwhelm the managers themselves when it comes time to track and report each metric on a routine basis. As a rule of thumb, organization-wide scorecards should be limited to roughly three to five metrics, especially during the initial introduction of a new program. Complicated scorecards consisting of a dozen or more metrics simply confuse the staff and send the message that "everything is important."

Some of the metrics discussed above tend to take care of themselves and may not require additional emphasis. Financial metrics will be routinely measured and reported by the corporate finance team. Most IT managers are already acutely aware of their significance and instinctively monitor their fluctuations. Furthermore, the number of individuals who can actually impact financial metrics is generally quite limited, since material buying decisions are restricted to the most senior members of the management team. Regulatory compliance metrics are monitored by audit teams and reported to the board of directors. It's unlikely they need additional emphasis unless the company operates within the financial services or health-care industries. Finally, business leaders are far more appropriate and far more qualified to report business metrics than their IT counterparts. IT should avoid preempting business leaders in measuring and reporting business results.

Other metrics may be vital to the operation or improvement of individual teams but may lack broader organizational significance. Some—such as information security metrics—may be too sensitive to include in scorecards that will be distributed widely across an organization.

All of these considerations underscore the difficulty of selecting metrics that can have a meaningful impact on organizational performance. Metrics programs have historically produced the greatest benefits when used to enhance the internal process discipline of an IT organization or support its strategic initiatives. For example, metrics programs are commonly launched to improve internal processes dealing with incident, problem, and change management; server provisioning; software quality management; and project management. Improvements in process discipline can have important downstream consequences as well. They can reduce internal rework, improve morale, and bolster the external credibility of the IT organization.

Overcoming Deming Denial: The Ultimate Metrics Frontier

Process discipline is a hard thing to instill in any human endeavor, but most IT shops exhibit an exceptional aversion to process management. It's ironic that the internal processes employed in so many other functions, such as sales, marketing, supply chain, and manufacturing, have become so sophisticated while many IT shops continue to fly by the seat of their pants, reacting to avoidable issues that are largely self-inflicted day after day after day.

William Edwards Deming pioneered the use of statistical methods to improve the quality of manufactured products by reducing the variability in process outcomes. Many attribute improvements in Japan's manufacturing capabilities during the second half of the twentieth century to the use of his techniques. Deming's methods laid the groundwork for the Six Sigma and Lean Manufacturing frameworks that became popular in the late 1990s and early 2000s. Unfortunately, these statistical control methods failed to take root within the IT industry. Most IT shops live in an ongoing state of "Deming Denial," lacking even the most elementary commitment to statistically based improvement programs.

Continuous performance improvement is an essential IT survival tactic in any large enterprise. End users and business executives take current performance levels for granted and constantly expect IT to operate better, faster, and cheaper in the future. Meanwhile, the financial stewards of the corporation continually pressure IT to reduce spending and limit head count growth. To avoid being torn apart by these two conflicting forces, IT organizations need to embrace Deming's techniques to continuously improve the consistency and quality of their internal processes. Metrics are the most readily available lever for institutionalizing the internal discipline that's required to maximize staff productivity, optimize the return on IT investments, and maintain desired levels of customer satisfaction. Properly designed and managed, metrics can cure the Deming Denial syndrome that plagues so many IT organizations.

Metrics programs are also powerful tools in aligning an organization around more strategic goals and objectives. Companies seeking to improve the online buying experience of their commercial customers by migrating revenue-generating systems to the cloud; or to expand their customer base by adapting legacy applications for use on mobile devices; or to accelerate product development by implementing DevOps techniques can all leverage targeted metrics to measure progress toward these transformational objectives. Irrespective of whether metrics are employed to improve organizational discipline or support strategic initiatives, they can play a constructive role in collapsing the spatial, temporal, and cultural differences that separate different teams within an IT organization. Effective metric programs provide a common language within the IT group and reinforce shared accountability for key dimensions of organizational performance. This benefit alone more than justifies their use!

It's all too easy for metrics initiatives to lose their novelty value and fade into the background of everyday business. Metrics scorecards should be reviewed regularly to ensure that they are still aligned with the critical dimensions of future organizational performance and that their individual components are critical levers for promoting desired behaviors. Healthy organizations outgrow individual metrics over time as they achieve the results that the metrics were initially designed to accomplish. Unhealthy organizations institutionalize selected metrics and allow them to persist long after they've outlived their usefulness or relevance.

In summary, metrics initiatives are loaded weapons. Properly aimed and deliberately managed, they can do much good. When they are haphazardly designed and casually managed, they can do great harm. Poorly designed initiatives send confusing signals to staff members about organizational priorities, trigger pointless debates about measurement procedures, waste inordinate time on meaningless data analysis activities, and ultimately undermine the internal credibility of the IT management team. Effective metrics campaigns require clarity regarding their objectives and sustained attention from their management sponsors. Ideally, every metric in a scorecard initiative should have a management champion who can vouch for its integrity and evangelize its significance throughout the organization.

How to Make Metrics Real?

Metrics can influence organizational behavior by their very existence. There's an old management saying: "Whatever interests my boss fascinates me." Managers who routinely review, react, celebrate, discuss, and display metric accomplishments will find that their teams are acutely aware of the performance objectives that the metrics were designed to address. These are the keys to making metrics real.

Review them. Metrics reviews should happen on a regular basis, ideally as part of other established management meetings and not as separate organizational exercises. The sponsor or champion of each metric should report on changes and trends. Such discussions should not be led by analysts who have no direct participation in the underlying processes that influence or control the outcome of a specific metric.

React to them. Talk is cheap. Do something about the metrics information you've received during the most recent review, especially if a metric is trending in the wrong direction. Convene a special meeting of relevant team members to discuss the reasons behind the apparent lapse in performance. Form a committee to solicit ideas for correcting the situation. Assign the issue to a key team member and make her responsible for identifying and correcting the underlying problem. In short, do something instead of accepting verbal explanations and assurances that the situation is under control. Emotional responses to performance lapses can be effective, provided they are not overused or overdramatized.

Celebrate them. Celebrate interim accomplishments whenever possible. Such celebrations don't have to be complicated or expensive. Put donuts in the coffee bar. Schedule a sports jersey day or favorite T-shirt day to underscore the significance of achieving a performance milestone. Offer to wear a wig to work on the day that an interim target is actually achieved and let the staff take selfies with you wearing the wig! Just do something out of the ordinary that's triggered by one or more metric accomplishments.

Discuss them informally. Incorporate metrics into your daily conversations with peers and staff members. Show them that your interest in organizational performance isn't limited to the monthly metrics review or the metrics scorecard presentation at the quarterly all-hands meeting. Exhibit genuine interest in why specific metrics have changed or congratulate a team member on the role she played in achieving an interim milestone. News of a manager's personal interest in specific metrics will spread rapidly throughout the IT team. Others will start paying attention to metric changes to ensure they're prepared for similar conversations with you in the future. Conventional wisdom suggests that you have to reward people with money to maintain their interest in metrics. Experience has shown that persistent management attention can have a much more profound and sustained effect if such attention is genuine.

Display them. You can't keep score without a scoreboard, and a scoreboard is pretty useless if it's not readily accessible. Once the mechanisms are in place to calculate metrics on a regular basis it should be relatively easy to display them as posters or video graphics throughout the organization.

Too many metrics programs are exercises in form over substance. Management teams churn out status reports on a regular basis and periodically share updates with staff members but no one can really remember what the metrics were originally designed to accomplish. Frankly, few staff members or first-line supervisors can even remember the individual metrics that are included in the program. Metrics programs can only succeed if the individuals who are most responsible for organizational performance—namely, the members of the management team—become personally invested in the program's execution. Managers need to exhibit genuine, visible, and persistent interest in their organization's key performance indicators and communicate the importance of such indicators to their teams. When you stop to think about it, that's really what they're supposed to be doing most of the time, anyway!

Chapter 6

Decoding Demand Signals from the Business

The goal of every IT organization is to furnish its business partners with the technical capabilities they need to increase their company's revenues and expand its profitability. To achieve these lofty goals, IT needs to develop a detailed understanding of the inner workings of individual business functions. More specifically, IT needs to be educated about the processes employed to support daily business operations, the challenges their functional colleagues encounter in performing their duties, and the nature of business initiatives being contemplated by functional leaders.

IT team members have very little insight into the issues and opportunities faced by their functional colleagues. Most have never worked outside the IT organization. The vast majority of IT staff members have never planned a marketing campaign, updated a sales opportunity, issued an inventory forecast, negotiated a contract, prepared an invoice, or processed a customer payment. Out of sheer necessity, all IT organizations are forced to establish intelligence-gathering systems to discover the operational challenges and business opportunities faced by their functional colleagues. IT prioritizes its support activities and spending plans on the basis of this business intelligence.

Information concerning the needs and plans of different business teams—hereafter referred to as "demand signals"—is generally obtained through three channels. Individual employees report their personal issues and requests to the IT service desk. Their needs are documented in the form of electronic trouble tickets that are dispatched to specialized technical teams for resolution. Functional teams construct prioritized lists of system enhancement requests and update such lists regularly, usually on a monthly or quarterly basis. Finally, business requests for major system upgrades or new capabilities are submitted to IT as formal project requests, ideally accompanied by business cases that document the benefits of proposed IT investments.

To summarize, the company's business needs are reported to IT through three primary channels: trouble tickets, enhancement lists, and project requests. Production support issues are also documented as trouble tickets, but are handled through separate processes outside these three demand channels. Informal demand mechanisms may exist within some smaller companies but as a company grows, business demand signals become increasingly confined to these three formal channels.

An IT group's performance and reputation are based upon the ways in which it responds to these business demands. Ninety percent of the employees within a company base their IT perceptions on the performance of the service desk. If IT is unable to resolve their problems or fulfill their requests in a timely fashion, they predictably develop negative perceptions regarding IT's technical competence, management capabilities, and work ethic. The remaining 10 percent of the employees are senior managers and executives. IT typically puts special processes in place to ensure their productivity issues and requests receive immediate attention. Their perceptions are largely based upon IT's project management capabilities. If IT is consistently unable to deliver project results on time and on budget, the company's leadership will predictably develop negative perceptions regarding IT's competence, capabilities, and work ethic.

IT management teams have a chronic tendency to focus their

attention on managing the perceptions of a company's business leaders at the expense of managing the perceptions of the other 90 percent of the employee population. Most management teams pay very little attention to the volume or nature of the tickets being recorded by the service desk. They are completely unaware of the top ten issues experienced by employees within a specific region or business unit or functional area. Nor do they monitor response or resolution times for various types of employee-submitted tickets. Sadly, it's quite easy for IT management teams to ignore demand signals channeled through the service desk. Employee-reported issues are rarely championed by senior business executives whose personal needs are being satisfied by a specialized set of VIP support processes. Consequently, the political cost of ignoring recurring employee complaints is usually quite small.

Failure to focus on recurring employee concerns results in a corresponding failure to focus the energy of the IT organization on resolving the root-cause issues responsible for such concerns. I have observed many situations in which IT deferred desktop upgrades, restricted access to selected systems, and enforced antiquated approval procedures simply because IT managers failed to appreciate the true level of pain their business colleagues were experiencing as a result of such issues. Employees are easily frustrated if the service desk is unable to address their concerns and will develop deep-seated negative impressions regarding the entire IT group if their needs are not met.

A continuous management focus on chronic employee frustrations can pay major dividends. It underscores IT's commitment to the success of its business colleagues and also showcases IT's technical competence. The goodwill generated through a consistent focus on recurring employee concerns can offset negative IT perceptions that inevitably occur when major projects run over schedule or over budget, or when IT has insufficient bandwidth to address specific enhancement or project requests. Enlightened IT leaders can stockpile some much-needed political capital by persistently focusing attention on the timely resolution of employee-reported concerns channeled through the service desk.

More complex demands for IT assistance are received through the enhancement and project request channels. These requests are usually constructed by operations teams embedded within individual corporate functions, such as sales, manufacturing, or distribution. Operations managers assigned to business units normally play a secondary role in planning system enhancements and formulating new IT initiatives. Their unit-specific needs are prioritized and consolidated by the corporate operations teams into enhancement or project requests that can satisfy the broadest possible cross section of enterprise needs.

Specific members of the operations teams are designated as lead points of contact for the IT group. These individuals assume responsibility for prioritizing enhancement requests within their function. They also play a primary role in planning major IT initiatives. They document the requirements for such initiatives and help build the business cases that justify future IT investments. These individuals—referred to as "super users" below—play a critical role in translating the needs of the business into terminology that IT can consume and act upon. Constructive working relationships with functional super users are essential to the success of any IT organization.

Demand signals received via the service desk are direct in nature. Individual company employees with specific needs or frustrations express their concerns directly to a member of the IT organization. Demand signals that appear as enhancement or project requests are indirect in nature. IT typically has little or no direct interaction with the individuals who will ultimately benefit from the completion of such requests.

Requests that are specifically designed to address the needs or desires of paying customers travel a particularly circuitous route before arriving at IT's doorstep. IT rarely has direct access to paying customers. Business colleagues in customer-facing functions such as marketing, sales, order management, professional services, and customer care have direct, firsthand experience dealing with the concerns, frustrations, needs, and desires of paying customers. Employees in these functions process such feedback through their own subjective lenses of personal experience and pass their perceptions and recommendations up their functional chain of command. Their viewpoints are compiled, distilled, and interpreted by the operations team supporting their function and ultimately relayed to IT in the form of enhancement and project requests.

Other functions, such as product development, manufacturing, and distribution, also obtain customer feedback, but in most cases their interactions with paying customers are also indirect in nature. They commonly infer customer needs without experiencing them directly. Other functions, such as finance, human resources, and procurement, primarily support internal customers. Their business demands are based on servicing their internal customers and maintaining compliance with external rules and regulations. Irrespective of the source, functional demands for IT assistance follow the same general procedure outlined above: prioritization within the function's operations team and communication to IT via the function's designated point of contact.

IT sits at the end of this tortuous pipeline with no direct interactions with the company's paying customers and no firsthand knowledge of the challenges facing individual functional groups. Demand signals that travel this pipeline can be modified in unpredictable ways by personal biases, inconsistent reporting, ad hoc compilation procedures, and the political agendas of various subgroups within the function. A cynic could legitimately question whether the enhancement and project requests that emerge through this process truly address the most critical issues and opportunities facing the corporation.

Beware the Super User

It's difficult for an IT professional to come to terms with the ugly truth that the majority of employees within their companies are just not all that "into" IT. This apathy extends from the most senior ranks of the company's management team to the junior ranks of entry-level employees. Employees view certain IT capabilities, such as email, file sharing, wifi connectivity, video conferencing, and remote application access, as fundamental utilities. They assume that the corporation is obligated to furnish these capabilities in much the same way that it's responsible for furnishing office space, conference rooms, printers, elevators, and parking facilities. Once their basic IT needs have been met, the vast majority of employees don't spend a lot of time or energy dreaming up creative new ways of leveraging IT capabilities within their teams or departments.

Business leaders are more inclined to explore ways of exploiting IT capabilities to improve the productivity or effectiveness of their teams. However, their intuitive interest in pursuing collaborative initiatives can be easily foiled by IT's incessant funding demands or the effort required to deal with the bureaucracy of the IT organization.

For some inexplicable reason, business leaders routinely suffer from the delusion that IT has discretionary resources that could be focused on their needs if they only spent a little more time with their IT peers. Conversely, IT leaders suffer from the delusion that business executives have discretionary funds that could be devoted to IT initiatives if the business and IT were only able to agree on the scope and nature of suitable IT investments. This delusional fog has inspired many unrewarding courtships. Both suitors believe that the object of their affection has disposable wealth that they would willingly share under the right circumstances, when in fact neither party has any discretionary resources whatsoever. Business leaders who have participated in one of these failed courtships are deeply disillusioned when they realize that their charm and attention have failed to dislodge discretionary IT resources, simply because there aren't any! Disillusioned business suitors are far less likely to devote time and effort to future discussions of IT initiatives after one of these failed courtships.

Business leaders can become equally frustrated by the effort required to deal with IT bureaucracy. An IT initiative that might seem simple or blatantly beneficial to a business leader will inevitably have to navigate the maze of IT's project approval and management procedures. A formal business case will be required to quantify potential costs and anticipated business benefits. If new software or hardware products are required, the procurement team will need to obtain competitive pricing from multiple vendors. If the initiative impacts regulated processes or sensitive data, SOX or PCI or HIPAA certification may be required. If the initiative involves critical revenue-generating systems, existing disaster recovery plans may need to be revised. If new devices or gateways are being added to the company's network, the information security team may need to approve the initiative's design. And the list goes on! Although each of these tasks serves a necessary purpose, the collective time and effort involved in moving from an initial idea to a new capability can exhaust the patience of even the most resilient executive. Business leaders are constantly being pressured to deliver short-term results, and they expect their IT counterparts to do likewise. If meaningful IT initiatives can't be accomplished within one or two quarters, many leaders will seriously question whether it's worth their time and energy to pursue them.

IT apathy can easily extend into the working ranks of a function or business unit as well. Employees outside IT already have full-time jobs. Their salary increases and cash bonuses are not based upon the time they spend working with the IT organization unless they're asked to do so by their managers. Consequently, they have very little instinctive motivation to collaborate with IT on future technology initiatives.

If the majority of business leaders and company employees lack the time, interest, or motivation to maintain an ongoing dialogue with the IT organization, who can IT leaders rely upon to stay informed about their customers' needs, challenges, and plans?

The dilemma of establishing some form of effective, ongoing communication between IT and its internal business clients is conventionally addressed through two highly complementary roles. Functional operations teams routinely designate a single individual to serve as their primary point of contact with the IT organization. This individual typically possesses in-depth understanding of the IT systems employed within their functional team. They may also have some type of technology background that further qualifies them for this role in the eyes of their coworkers. There's no commonly accepted title for individuals serving in this critical liaison role. I refer to them as "super users." IT problems and requests emanating from individual functional areas are routinely escalated to IT's attention through these super users. Correspondingly, IT designates an individual who can work with super users to translate functional issues and demands into technical specifications that can be addressed by the IT organization. Individuals performing this role are commonly referred to as business systems analysts (BSAs).

Super users tend to be highly regarded by members of the IT organization because they provide valuable business information that's difficult to obtain through other channels. However, the converse is not always true. Super users are not necessarily held in equally high regard by their functional colleagues. Many individuals in functional roles view their dealings with IT as necessary but unrewarding busywork that distracts them from their principal duties. Some, if not most, functional colleagues would view a super user assignment with trepidation, as more of a punishment than a career development opportunity. Individuals who are attracted to the role may have a personal affinity for technology that places them far outside the mainstream of their colleagues' interests. IT organizations need to beware of becoming overly reliant on super users because they may not be trusted or influential members of their function's leadership team.

Super User Credibility

In a past life, my IT group routinely supported our company's annual sales kickoff meeting by establishing a PC clinic at the kickoff hotel. Participants were encouraged to drop their PCs off at the clinic, where they would be inspected, cleaned, and updated as necessary. Hundreds of PCs were serviced in this fashion during the meeting. The attendees sincerely appreciated the personalized treatment they received, and IT always received multiple compliments for providing the service.

One year, I decided to expand our participation in the kickoff meeting by setting up a series of display booths that highlighted new IT capabilities of potential interest to the field sales representatives. The sales operations team learned of our plans and decided they would join us and set up some display booths of their own in the same general location. Over the course of the meeting, I was shocked to observe that foot traffic at the IT booths exceeded traffic at the sales operations booths by a factor of three or four. The individuals manning the sales operations booths were the super users we worked with on a regular basis. It was quite obvious that the super users had very few personal relationships with members of the field sales team because so few stopped by, even to chat on a casual basis. I had always assumed that our key contacts in sales operations had close working relationships with their field sales colleagues. I had frankly treated them as surrogates for the field sales representatives. My experiences at the kickoff meeting demonstrated that this was clearly not the case, and led me to question the credibility of super users in other functions as well.

The personal interests, experiences, and concerns of a super user can significantly impact the guidance he provides to IT, sometimes consciously and sometimes unconsciously. Super users may be unduly influenced by frustrations they experienced with specific IT systems earlier in their careers. They may send IT off to address their historical frustrations, even if they're only marginally relevant to current business operations. Super users can become obsessively focused on customizing key systems to address exceptional business situations that occur infrequently at the expense of automating more commonly performed tasks. By definition, super users are the most proficient users of the IT systems supporting their individual functional areas. Consciously or subconsciously, they tend to promote enhancements and new capabilities that would make other users like themselves more productive. They can easily lose sight of the frustrations and productivity issues that less proficient members of their teams experience on a daily basis. It's not uncommon for system enhancements requested by super users to go unused after implementation simply because their functional colleagues lack the ability or sophistication to leverage highly specialized enhancements.

Conscientious super users recognize the limitations of their personal experience and IT knowledge, and choose to operate as facilitators. They educate BSAs about the internal business practices within their function. They selectively recruit business colleagues to assist in prioritizing IT requests and formulating IT initiatives. They are willing to explore alternative technical solutions to functional needs.

Dictatorial super users view themselves as the "single source of truth" regarding the opportunities and challenges faced by their functional teams. They are not interested in wasting the time of their colleagues in prioritizing requests and planning initiatives, since they believe they are fully capable of performing such tasks on their own. They may also believe that they have sufficient technical knowledge to function as solution architects and will not only tell IT what to do but how to do it. Dictatorial super users expect the IT organization to comply with their requests and follow their direction with minimal discussion or debate.

Unfortunately, many IT organizations fall into the trap of letting super users become their principal, and sometimes exclusive, point of contact with different functional teams. This strategy represents the path of least resistance from the perspective of IT management, but it inevitably limits the depth and breadth of ongoing communication with

IT's business clients. Many IT leaders have had to learn the hard way that pleasing super users doesn't necessarily improve IT's credibility or stature within the functional groups they serve. Enlightened IT leaders cultivate multiple communication channels with individual functional groups that complement the feedback and direction being supplied by the super users.

Super Users As Roadblocks

Earlier in my career, my IT group supported the operations of a 24×7 customer call center that employed more than eight hundred agents. The call center was housed in a separate facility located some distance from corporate headquarters. It had no on-site IT technicians. The center experienced a steady stream of infrastructure and application issues, many of which required vendor assistance to resolve. The tension between the center's management team and IT grew week by week as problems continued to occur, and all that IT could do was to escalate its pleas for vendor assistance. The technical issues involved in this situation were rapidly overtaken by emotional concerns. Rightly or wrongly, the call center managers concluded that IT didn't really care about their problems and that they were consistently receiving second-class treatment from the IT team.

In an attempt to soothe frayed nerves, I conscripted a tiger team of IT specialists and devoted them to the call center's issues for a sixty-day period. Tiger team members were expected to work at the center during this assignment. The team's goal was to fix as many problems as possible during the sixty days they were on site. The call center managers were euphoric when presented with this proposal. The one person who though it was a crazy idea that served no useful purpose was...the super user, of course. The call center's super user told me that she had already documented all the issues that needed to be addressed and that deploying IT staff members to the call center was a complete waste of time. We proceeded anyway and, not surprisingly, the entire exercise was a huge success. The tiger team spent the first week sitting deskside with the call agents, observing their use of various applications and databases. Infrastructure team members ran a variety of diagnostic tests on the center's call routing system and other related equipment. Based upon these experiences, the team identified a series of fixes that could be implemented in successive waves. Anything that took longer than sixty days to implement was deemed to be a project and needed to compete for resources through the normal project approval process.

Although we intentionally involved the super user in reviewing the team's action plan and we liberally shared credit for the success of the exercise with her, it was quite clear that she was shocked that we felt the need to work directly with her colleagues to learn more about the issues that were impeding their productivity. She had become quite comfortable serving as the "single source of truth" regarding the IT needs of her function and did not appreciate our efforts to develop a deeper understanding of their frustrations and concerns.

Revenge of the Business Systems Analysts

There are few roles within IT that are more valuable and yet more consistently underappreciated than that of the business system analyst. BSAs are assigned to individual business functions. They spend the majority of their time working with functional leaders and staff members. They become intimately familiar with the business processes performed within a function and directly observe ways in which existing IT systems are used to support daily operations. They provide a critical two-way interface between IT and its business partners. They translate functional needs into IT requirements and lobby for initiatives that will improve the productivity of their functional clients.

Successful BSAs develop constructive working relationships with one or more super users within their assigned function. BSAs and super users typically share a common in-depth understanding of the systems supporting the function's current business processes. The super user possesses a deeper understanding of the function's role in the company's overall business model, how it interacts with other functional departments, and the challenges faced by its members. The BSA possesses a deeper technical understanding of IT systems supporting the function and the operational practices IT employs to maintain those systems.

Super users and BSAs work in close collaboration to prioritize system enhancements. Super users prioritize functional needs from a business perspective, while BSAs are able to estimate the time and effort required to implement specific functional requests. Prioritized lists of desired system enhancements are invariably based upon a trade-off between functional benefits and available IT resources.

Super users and BSAs also work closely in implementing new IT capabilities. BSAs take the lead in testing and validating new capabilities before they are fully implemented. Super users are typically responsible for the end-user training required to fully adopt new capabilities.

Ideally, super users and BSAs should form highly complementary and highly collaborative partnerships. They each bring unique knowledge and experiences to the partnership, they share common goals, and they can produce greater benefits as a team than as individuals. BSAs should possess the business acumen, technical knowledge, and interpersonal skills needed to question and challenge some of the requests presented by their functional clients. They should be able to question whether the benefits associated with specific requests are worth the effort required for their implementation. They should be able to challenge the utility of other proposals because similar requests implemented in the past have failed to be adopted in practice or failed to produce anticipated results. In short, BSAs should operate as proverbial "trusted advisors" to the functions they support, ensuring that the functions are obtaining the maximum benefits from the IT resources they are receiving.

In reality, BSAs rarely establish a true partnership-of-equals relationship with their super user counterparts. In some instances, BSAs lack the business knowledge, technical insight, or influencing skills to challenge business requests in a constructive fashion. In other instances, critical feedback is not welcomed by the super user and the super user will use her idiosyncratic knowledge of functional practices to trump any challenges or suggestions presented by her BSA partners. Super users typically possess greater political capital and positional authority than BSAs, which can further limit a BSA's ability to push back on specific requests or proposals.

BSAs who offer an independent perspective and fail to act as order takers are commonly labeled as being "difficult to work with" or "not a team player." Their annual performance ratings suffer as a consequence, and they soon learn to respond to functional requests in an unquestioning manner. More often than not, super user–BSA relationships deteriorate into partnerships of unequals, in which the BSA is clearly operating in a subservient role.

The advent of SaaS applications changes the super user–BSA relationship in some fundamental and perhaps revolutionary ways. When a company's business application portfolio consisted almost exclusively of homegrown applications or commercially licensed software, BSAs functioned as co-conspirators (either willingly or unwillingly) in the endless customization of business systems. No business whim or preference was too unique or too arcane to be rejected by subservient BSAs.

Significant IT effort was devoted to enhancements and bolt-on systems that addressed the desires of isolated functional subteams or infrequently encountered business situations. SaaS applications preempt such customization efforts.

Customization of SaaS applications is difficult to achieve and expensive to maintain. SaaS companies implement new functionality frequently, sometimes on a weekly, monthly, or quarterly basis. Maintaining unique customizations within or outside a SaaS application is a nightmare that actually distracts a company from exploiting the steady stream of new capabilities being introduced by the SaaS vendor.

In a SaaS-dominated environment, functional organizations no longer change business applications to suit their processes—*they adjust their processes to leverage the capabilities of the SaaS applications.* This shift in approach can significantly expand the influence and impact of BSAs. BSAs who develop an in-depth understanding of individual SaaS applications and have modest process reengineering skills are positioned to have a much greater impact on the future success of their functional clients. In a SaaS-dominated environment, business changes are no longer limited by the speed at which IT can implement new capabilities. Rather, they are limited by the function's ability to change its internal practices and procedures. BSAs will be spending considerably less time prioritizing lists of system enhancements and customizations in the future. They will be spending considerably more time assisting super users in redesigning functional processes and retraining functional staff members. Super users will become increasingly dependent upon BSAs to ensure that their function is realizing the greatest possible benefits from its SaaS subscription fees.

BSAs have been relegated to second-class-citizen status in too many IT organizations for too long. They've habitually deferred to the desires and whims of their super user partners and been held in low regard by their own IT colleagues. With the appropriate training in process reengineering techniques and SaaS application workflows, BSAs can exert considerably more influence within their client groups and materially enhance the business impact of the overall IT team. It would be criminal not to provide the training they need to seek their revenge in this brave, new SaaS-dominated world!

Beware the Back-Office Trap

IT organizations are commonly considered to be back-office functions similar to finance, human resources, procurement, and facilities. This can have a subtle but persistent impact on the way in which IT prioritizes demand signals from different functional teams.

In some companies, IT reports to a COO or CFO or CAO (chief administrative officer) who is responsible for one or more additional back-office functions as well. In these situations, it's difficult not to place a higher priority on back-office demands emanating from peer organizations at the expense of the needs of front-office or customer-facing functions. IT organizations grouped with other back-office functions gradually become more attuned to the needs of their peers and inevitably seek praise from their common boss by keeping their peers happy. This subliminal prioritization of back-office demands can become overt if the common boss periodically intervenes on behalf of the other organizations under his control and explicitly requests special treatment for their requests.

The back-office trap is far less common in companies in which the IT function reports directly to the CEO. Under these circumstances, the CIO functions as a peer of all the other functional executives and it's much easier to treat disparate functional demands on an evenhanded basis. When this is not the case, IT leaders need to become exceptionally proactive in fostering ongoing communication with front-office functions and ensuring that their needs are being properly prioritized.

The prioritization of back-office demands over those emanating from front-office functions—whether intentional or subliminal—may produce some short-term political benefits at the expense of longer-term political risks. Experience has shown that when companies face adverse business conditions, the leaders of front-office functions generally have more influence in determining how painful budget cuts and staffing reductions will be distributed. If they feel they've been under-served by IT in the past, they will be far less likely to shield IT from traumatic cutbacks in current spending or staffing levels.

Chapter 7

Exercising the Power of Position

Why do so many individuals who work so hard to achieve IT leadership roles continue to perform many aspects of their old jobs when they are promoted into positions of greater responsibility? Many emerging leaders have an almost obsessive focus on career advancement. Yet when they are promoted into a role with broad leadership potential they fail to use it as a developmental opportunity and largely ignore the prerogatives associated with their new position.

The routine activities that occur within IT organizations can exert a subliminal gravitational attraction on the attention of their leaders. There are a myriad of operational issues, project planning activities, vendor selection exercises, financial reviews, contract negotiations, and personnel issues that occur with monotonous regularity within every IT shop. Leaders need to play a selective role in shaping and overseeing routine activities. They need to scrupulously avoid becoming an active participant in most of them. Just because a leader has relevant technical knowledge or organizational experience to contribute to any of these activities, she doesn't necessarily need to become personally involved in their conduct or completion.

Leaders who play an active role in routine activities do themselves and their teams a grave disservice. It's impossible for team members to obtain the developmental experiences they need to advance in their careers if the leader is continually directing what, when, where, and how work will be performed. Furthermore, the leader's participation in such activities distracts her from exercising the unique prerogatives associated with her position. Failure to leverage these prerogatives will compromise her team's ability to improve its internal productivity and business impact. Sadly, leaders who are unable to overcome the congenital compulsion to perform one or more of their past jobs in their current role will find their own career prospects severely limited.

The Search for Objective Reality

Most human organizations construct a set of reinforcing beliefs regarding their character, behavior, and accomplishments. This belief system generally casts the organization in the most positive possible light and serves as a source of inspiration and motivation for its members. It can also serve as a survival mechanism when the organization comes under attack or criticism.

This phenomenon is readily observable in most companies. Companies routinely convince themselves that they have developed superior products, hired the best sales team, constructed the most efficient manufacturing facilities, made the shrewdest acquisitions, nurtured the happiest employees, etc. They continually reinforce these beliefs until they receive an unsolicited buyout offer from a private equity firm that believes the company has lost its competitive edge through gross mismanagement! The private equity firm employs the same empirica data that's available to the company's employees and leaders but dra very different conclusions regarding the company's character, beha and accomplishments.

IT organizations encase themselves in similar sets of rein beliefs. It's generally quite possible to find a variety things "going right" within an IT group. Perhaps your team has just negotiated a 20 percent discount on a renewal contract with a major vendor. Perhaps you've reduced the time required to provision a virtual server from one day to one hour. Perhaps a senior business executive has sent you a particularly nice note congratulating your service desk team on the treatment he received during a recent overseas trip. These experiences and many, many others can readily create the perception that "we're doing pretty well" in terms of our team's overall performance.

All of the hypothetical events referenced above could take place without the organization realizing that it's still paying a 25 percent premium for the vendor product relative to other companies of similar size, that other shops are provisioning virtual servers in ten minutes instead of one hour, and that key members of the company's sales team are wholly dissatisfied with the performance of the service desk. Someone has to pierce the protective shell of self-congratulatory beliefs that organizations naturally construct and expose their members to objective truths, no matter how painful those truths may be. That is the responsibility of every IT leader.

Effective leaders proactively seek ways of bridging the chasm between internal belief systems and objective reality. Objective reality regarding an organization's effectiveness can be obtained in many different ways. It can be obtained by reaching out to business executives at more senior levels in the company to obtain their perceptions about the performance of the IT organization. In the example given above, the leader of the service desk team could contact three regional sales managers and ask them to share any anecdotal stories they have recently heard regarding his team's performance. Alternatively, the leader could simply inquire about the sales managers' general perceptions regarding the support they have been receiving from his team, since perception *is* reality within the sales community.

External consultants and suppliers can also assist in gauging the efficiency of internal operations. Third-party research firms may possess benchmark information regarding the efficiency of many standard

IT processes. Vendors routinely publish case studies describing efficiencies other companies have achieved through the use of their products. Unfortunately, information obtained through benchmark firms and vendor case studies can raise more questions than it answers. Almost invariably, additional information is needed regarding the manner in which the reference data was collected and analyzed before any concrete conclusions can be drawn regarding the efficiency of the leader's organization.

The most straightforward means of assessing the efficiency of internal practices is simply to visit other IT shops with similar operational challenges. Many shops are willing to host best-practice discussions, provided the companies involved are not in direct business competition. The scope and ground rules for such an information exchange need to be established on a leader-to-leader basis. If leaders don't possess the professional network or personal initiative needed to instigate such discussions, they will never occur. It's ironic that many IT leaders would rather conduct three meetings with a vendor to plan a benchmark study, pay the vendor $50,000, and then conduct three more meetings trying to interpret the study results before they would ever think of picking up the phone and calling their counterpart at another company to compare current practices!

Objective reality is a particularly valuable commodity in evaluating the claims of competing vendors. Most IT shops employ proof-of-concept exercises or trial subscriptions to validate vendor claims. Broader insights can frequently be obtained by conducting reference calls with some of the vendor's existing customers, attending vendor user-group meetings, reviewing anecdotal comments captured in social collaboration tools, and proactively visiting current users of the vendor's product. The richest information exchange typically occurs during face-to-face visits with existing customers where it's possible to have a true dialog about the implementation issues, support requirements, and business benefits associated with the use of the vendor's product.

If IT leaders spend the majority of their time micromanaging the work activities of their teams, the outreach efforts described above will never occur. In the absence of these efforts, the organization will continue to encase itself in a series of self-congratulatory beliefs and waste countless hours re-creating information regarding vendor capabilities that is already common knowledge within the industry. This is the disservice that leaders impose upon their teams when they fail to exercise their positional prerogatives to initiate outreach efforts beyond the boundaries of the IT organization.

CEOs provide a graphic illustration of this phenomenon. CEOs achieve their leadership positions in a variety of ways. Some have financial backgrounds and have functioned as CFOs before they ascended to the CEO throne. Others had illustrious careers in sales or manufacturing before being promoted into a CEO role. Almost inevitably, first-time CEOs continue to focus undue attention on the performance of the functions or business units from which they came, at the expense of spending time with key external constituencies such as board members, financial analysts, major investors, and the industry trade press. Seasoned CEOs use their time very differently. Not only do they spend time with the constituencies referenced above, they sit on the boards of other companies to obtain insights regarding current business trends. They expand their network of personal contacts with other CEOs, both within and outside their industries, and use information gleaned from such contacts to shape their companies' business strategies. In short, they back away from the routine operational activities that are ultimately the responsibility of their direct reports to do the things that they are uniquely able to do in their CEO roles.

IT leaders should take lessons from the behaviors of seasoned CEOs. All IT leaders should reflect on the positional prerogatives that accompany their role and exercise the power of their positions to obtain the objective external information that will ultimately make them and their team more productive and more effective. There are certain forms of outreach that only the leader can initiate, and if the leader does not pursue such efforts, his team will suffer as a consequence.

Time Management Test

Many readers of this chapter may be tempted to think about the steady stream of meetings that fill their weekly calendars and conclude that they are already spending considerable time outside the confines of their offices and conference rooms. There's an easy way to test that assertion. Print your monthly calendar and get two highlighters of different colors. Highlight meetings with internal business leaders in one color and highlight meetings with vendors or professional colleagues outside the company in a different color. (Teleconferences or phone calls can be treated as meetings for the purposes of this exercise.) If you work in a company that suffers from meeting mania, you might circle meetings with internal business leaders that were not regularly scheduled meetings (i.e., meetings that were initiated by you or a business leader for a specific purpose). What fraction of the month did you devote to external interactions with vendors or professional colleagues? What's the ratio of external meetings to internal meetings? What's the ratio of circled internal meetings to all internal meetings? Are you still convinced that you are fully exercising the power of your position?

Even individuals who have the interest and inclination to obtain objective information from internal business leaders and external colleagues will find that the gravitational forces of everyday work restrict the time they are able to spend outside their own organizations. Finding time to exercise the power of position is a constant battle, but it is a battle that true leaders fight and win every month. Outreach efforts should take precedence over many other activities competing for a leader's time and attention simply because leaders are the only members of their organization who are fully licensed to conduct such efforts.

Overcoming Organizational Narcissism

IT leaders need to seriously contemplate the personal motivations that keep them mired in their offices and conference rooms, interacting constantly—sometime exclusively—with the members of their own staff. Some may enjoy the sense of power and control they experience by constantly inserting themselves into routine activities. Some may enjoy the intellectual gratification associated with the use of their knowledge and experience to determine the best outcome for every task or activity. Others may be so concerned about the limitations of their team members that they deem it necessary to personally compensate for their team's skill gaps. If a leader's technical or operational expertise is needed to make the majority of decisions within their team or to serve as their team's chief quality control officer, then the leader has the wrong team! No leader, regardless of her dedication, work ethic, or intelligence, has the time or energy required to compensate for pervasive skill gaps on a sustained basis.

Some leaders may refrain from initiating outreach efforts because they are socially inept and find it awkward to initiate conversations with casual acquaintances or strangers. Some may suffer from poor time management and allow the members of their team to control how they use their time instead of controlling it themselves. Others may simply be lazy. They may believe that leaders are supposed to work less than individual contributors and choose to rest on their laurels as a reward for their past accomplishments.

Leaders who seek promotion into broader management roles need to analyze and acknowledge the personal motivations that are limiting the frequency and effectiveness of their outreach efforts, and take intentional steps to overcome such motivations. To paraphrase the opening lines of the *Star Trek* TV series, all aspiring IT leaders should be encouraged to "go boldly where few IT leaders have gone before." Instead of seeking strange new worlds, the leader might benefit from attending a quarterly sales review, taking a peer at another company out to lunch to discuss storage management practices, or scheduling a Skype call with a vendor product manager to provide direct feedback about a critical tool being employed in daily operations. If the leader fails to exercise the power of her position to initiate these types of outreach efforts, they will never occur. Both the leader and her team will be shortchanged as a consequence.

Distant View of the Paying Customer

The most beneficial outreach effort any leader can undertake is to establish direct contact with their company's paying customers. Most IT organizations have a very distant view of the customers who are actually procuring their company's products and services. Feedback from paying customers arrives at IT's doorstep through a tortuous process involving customer care systems, fellow employees in customer-facing roles, and functional operations teams. If an IT leader is able to circumvent these internal intermediaries and obtain direct customer feedback through email, text, phone, video, or face-to-face conversations, he should always seize the opportunity to do so. An IT leader armed with objective truth regarding the perceptions and buying experiences of paying customers will be far better equipped to fend off ill-advised requests for application enhancements or infrastructure changes from internal business partners. In addition, he will be in a far better position to propose initiatives that can truly improve the experience and satisfaction of the individuals who are ultimately underwriting the expenses of the IT organization.

Chapter 8

Managing Innovation

When IT employees are asked what they like most about their jobs, many will tell you they like working in a profession in which everything is constantly changing. This is absolutely true. IT sits at the crossroads between the evolving needs of its business partners and the perpetual innovation that occurs within the technology industry. IT should ideally serve as the spark plug for technology innovation within an enterprise, collaborating with its partners in implementing new capabilities that will improve the efficiency of daily operations and deliver competitive business advantages as well.

Innovation plays a particularly critical role in continuously improving the performance of an IT organization. Internal innovation is not limited to the introduction of new technology. People and process changes can also have a major impact on an organization's efficiency and effectiveness. Significant innovation can be achieved simply by hiring individuals with skills and experiences that differ from those of existing team members. New recruits frequently find ways of improving organizational performance by wringing additional benefits out of existing processes and technologies. In other instances, the quality of IT services can be improved through organizational changes in which dedicated teams are formed to support critical business functions such as sales or manufacturing. Process innovation can also produce significant benefits without necessarily changing the skill mix or technologies within an IT organization. Six Sigma initiatives routinely produce benefits without requiring new IT capabilities or significant changes to existing systems or infrastructure. Without intending to downplay the importance of people-driven or process-driven innovation, this chapter focuses specifically on the third source of innovation: technology.

Technology innovation is an inescapable force of nature within the IT industry. It changes careers. It can bankrupt historical investment decisions. It can revolutionize a company's internal practices or transform its business strategies. Demands for new technical capabilities exist within all large enterprises, in both the best of times and the worst of times. Even when revenues are down and budgets are tight, advances in the price/performance of IT hardware or the sophistication of key software applications will be more than sufficient to justify new technology investments.

The landscape of technological innovation has changed dramatically during the past decade. The number of new technology providers has increased exponentially, while barriers to procurement and adoption have been lowered. Without some form of governance or oversight, these changes can lead to technology chaos within any large enterprise.

As little as ten to fifteen years ago, large IT vendors such as IBM, Hewlett-Packard, Cisco, Microsoft, SAP, and Oracle were the principal agents of innovation within the IT industry. Venture capitalists (VCs) have displaced the mega-vendors and assumed this role by underwriting the creation of thousands of start-up companies. The Darwinian competition of new ideas within the VC community is extensive and intense. VCs make investments that are intended to revolutionize different aspects of the IT industry, while entrenched vendors make R&D investments that will protect and expand their existing revenue streams. Mega-vendors have been unable to compete with the creativity and ubiquity of their start-up competitors and commonly resort to acquiring start-ups to avoid irrelevance in the current IT marketplace.

Freeware tools and consumer technologies further multiply the technology choices available to a modern enterprise. A wide variety of freeware capabilities have matured to a point where they are enterprise-ready, and a host of other open source tools are rapidly reaching that stage. Mobile applications, file-sharing services, and collaboration tools that were initially designed for consumer use are being widely adopted by small work groups to conduct company business. In fact, as conventional application vendors race to adapt their products to mobile platforms, the distinctions between consumer applications and business applications are becoming quite blurry for many mobile users.

IT's ability to control the introduction of new technologies within an enterprise was easier in the past, when the acquisition process involved large capital expenditures and complex contract negotiations. These types of expenditures required formal approval processes and IT typically took the lead in ensuring that such processes were properly executed. These formal control procedures have been seriously eroded by the widespread availability of cloud-based subscription services, freeware, and consumer technologies.

Cloud services can be initially adopted on a very limited scale and subsequently expanded on a pay-as-you-go basis. They don't require capital investments and can be procured by functional departments using discretionary expense budgets that are outside IT's purview. Consumer technologies are also commonly adopted on a limited scale by individual work groups and are largely subsidized by the company's employees themselves. And freeware is... well, free! All of these factors combine to significantly lower the barriers to entry of many new types of technology within a large enterprise.

The challenge facing every IT leadership team is whether they are going to manage technology innovation or be victimized by it in the current environment of expanded choice and lower entry barriers. Victimization occurs when innovation proceeds with no management direction or oversight. If new technologies are implemented in a haphazard fashion based upon the parochial interests of IT's vendors, customers, or staff members, the organization will end up with an unwieldy portfolio of capabilities that is difficult to operate and costly to maintain. The relevant question is not *whether* technology innovation will be allowed to occur but rather *how* it will be managed by IT in the future. Pressures to adopt new technology typically originate from external vendors, internal business clients, and members of the IT staff. All three of these innovation forces need to be proactively managed if IT hopes to retain its role as the leader of technology change within the enterprise.

Vendor-Driven Innovation

Vendors make money and grow their businesses by selling new things. More specifically, the incentive programs employed by most vendors reward their field sales representatives for selling new products and services. Sales incentive programs provide little, if any, reward for the renewal of existing contracts. Every interaction that occurs between a vendor and an IT organization is fundamentally motivated by the vendor's desire to expand current sales levels, either in the short term or long term.

The enterprise IT marketplace is large and lucrative. Vendors operating in this marketplace don't randomly approach prospective customers with a canned sales pitch. They conduct sophisticated campaigns employing a mixture of relationship development, technical education, and competitor bashing that is tailored for each prospective customer. Their efforts are as comprehensive as they are insidious. They cultivate personal relationships through dinners, wine tastings, golf outings, and sporting events. They promote technical education through briefings, trial subscriptions, proof-of-concept experiments, user group meetings, reference calls with existing customers, etc. And finally they rarely miss an opportunity to spread fear, uncertainty, and doubt about their competitors. They inoculate existing customers with a limited number of free capabilities, hoping the customer will use such capabilities on an operational basis and buy more (not for free) during the next contract renewal cycle. They increase maintenance fees on legacy investments to goad customers into buying new capabilities as a cost savings measure, or offer financial incentives such as free consulting support or deferred fees on new purchases. Vendors selling into new accounts will fly IT managers to their corporate headquarters for customized briefings, flaunt their most recent "new logo" customers, brag about the source of their venture capital funds (if still private), and generally try to make IT leaders feel that they are joining an exclusive club of enlightened executives if they adopt the vendor's latest and greatest product offering.

Enterprise IT vendors—whether entrenched mega-vendors or new start-ups—employ sales professionals who have honed their skills through years of practice. They have tried-and-true playbooks of sales inducements to convince prospective customers that they cannot live without the vendor's new capabilities. Each of the inducements referenced above is relatively innocuous in its own right. Collectively, they can become an overwhelming force, driving an IT organization to embrace the innovation strategies of its vendors.

Customer-Driven Innovation

Have you ever heard the story about the business executive who falls in love with some type of new technology after talking to a friend, attending a meeting, or reading an in-flight airline magazine? Such stories are essential parts of the historical folklore of every IT organization. They're shared for purposes of amusement or entertainment, but they continue to happen with alarming frequency and their ramifications are deadly serious. Examples abound. The marketing group discovers a new lead-scoring tool; HR learns about a cool applicant-tracking application; internal audit becomes obsessed with a new controls-management system; a board member recommends a currency trading application to the CFO; and they all arrive on IT's doorstep asking IT to simply "make it happen." Political considerations can easily trump technical or contractual issues when such initiatives receive strong personal endorsements from key business executives. Any concerns IT may have regarding the implementation, operation, or maintenance of a customer-selected technology will be further marginalized if the sponsoring executive has the necessary funding to purchase the designated product himself.

As discussed above, consumer technologies can make even stealthier inroads into large enterprises. The introduction of such technologies doesn't necessarily require the support or endorsement of business leaders. It can occur when members of a project team, work group, or small department decide to leverage texting tools, file sharing systems, data feeds, project management freeware, or other tools to manage their daily activities. Information security teams within large enterprises discover hundreds of these types of technologies when they scan Internet traffic on their company's network.

Staff-Driven Innovation

IT leaders are frequently unaware of the fifth column technology movements occurring within the bowels of their own organizations. Every member of the IT staff is a technologist, and each has his own unique set of past work experiences, past vendor relationships, professional colleagues, personal friends, and family members. Each is exposed to a steady stream of new product ideas, suggestions, and solicitations through one or more of these channels. Recently hired staff members commonly extol the virtues of the tools they employed in their former jobs and may lobby strenuously for their use in their current positions. Existing employees may download freeware tools, subscribe to new services on a trial basis, or obtain access to vendor sandbox environments without incurring any appreciable costs and without the knowledge of their supervisors. In other instances, supervisors may provide tacit approval simply to avoid conflict and keep their team members happy. These types of "selection decisions" are completely ad hoc and don't address the cost, reliability, redundancy, interoperability, and security concerns that would be considered in formally evaluating a new technology.

In the absolute worst-case scenario, enterprise innovation is being driven by all three of these constituencies with no management oversight or direction. The cumulative cost and risk associated with unmanaged innovation is staggering. First of all, staff members and lower-level supervisors can waste inordinate amounts of time on vendor presentations, trial subscriptions, and experimental deployments of new products that will never be utilized on an enterprise basis due to cost, risk, prioritization issues, or organizational adoption barriers. If new technologies obtain a toehold position in certain portions of the enterprise, more time will be wasted trying to integrate them with existing products that possess similar or overlapping capabilities. In many instances, new products offered by emerging companies have not been widely deployed within large enterprises. Consequently, they may not "play nicely" with complementary or competing products and may actually degrade the performance, corrupt the databases, or trigger the outages of key systems.

Finally, even if sufficient funding exists and implementation and integration concerns can be resolved, a constant influx of new products and services resulting from vendor sales pressures, business partner infatuations, and the staff's fifth column initiatives will produce an exceedingly complex technology portfolio that will become increasingly difficult to operate and maintain. Managed innovation is the only means of avoiding this dilemma.

Managing an Innovation Pipeline

Some might argue that the term "managed innovation" is an oxymoron. Many cling to the romantic notion that innovation is—by definition—a form of uncontrolled, unmanaged, and unanticipated change that springs from the grassroots of an organization. While that may be true for basic research or university-based R&D programs, it is not the way that innovation typically occurs within a commercial enterprise.

IT organizations have tried to manage technology innovation in many different ways. Some establish skunkworks programs or innovation labs in which new capabilities can be explored informally with minimal management oversight. Others stage employee hackathons to develop prototypical business applications that exploit new technical capabilities. Still others sponsor incubator programs in which small teams are granted dedicated time and resources to construct more complex applications or systems. Predictably, management's role in sanctioning these various activities is directly proportional to the time and resources involved. The barriers to hackathon participation are commonly quite minimal, while participation in an incubator program typically occurs through a competitive proposal process overseen by management.

All of these programs have merit but they do not necessarily address the full range of innovation pressures and clandestine initiatives created by the three forces discussed above. IT managers generally operate at the pinnacle of an "iceberg of innovation" occurring within the enterprise. Formal programs that are highly visible tend to mask the much broader range of research activities taking place without the knowledge or approval of the IT management team.

IT management needs to find a judicious means of exposing the full range of exploratory activities being conducted across the IT organization to accelerate initiatives that have potential value and terminate those that do not. IT leaders need to establish organization-wide transparency for all evaluation and prototyping activities to ensure that relevant stakeholders are involved at appropriate points in time, that the effort being devoted to individual activities is commensurate with their likelihood of success, and that initiatives of questionable value or low likelihood of implementation are terminated as soon as possible.

Managed innovation occurs through a progressive chain of activities in which new or unconventional ideas receive increasing attention and validation from the IT organization as a whole and from the IT management team in particular. Unconventional ideas become interesting leads, leads become viable prospects, and prospects become recognized opportunities through this chain of events. This pipeline of activities distills a broad array of interesting ideas into a handful of validated opportunities that merit investment and adoption. It bears a striking resemblance to the pipeline management practices of sales organizations that similarly distill a broad array of sales leads into a much smaller subset of closed deals.

IT leaders face the dual challenges of establishing sufficient transparency in the management of their pipeline and sufficient trust within their organizations to encourage the participation of all team members in the innovation process. This is a delicate balancing act that must nurture creativity while minimizing wasted effort. It requires persistent communication across all levels of the organization. It's ultimately the responsibility of the CIO and his leadership team. The mechanics of the pipeline management process can be facilitated by a CTO or an enterprise architecture group, but responsibility for moving individual ideas through the pipeline cannot be delegated to a single individual or group. Innovation management should be one of the primary responsibilities of every IT leadership team. Properly executed, it should also be one of the most fun.

Disciplined sales organizations establish specific gating criteria to change the status of a potential customer from lead to prospect to opportunity. These criteria involve such things as identifying a champion within the potential account, conducting an on-site workshop or product demonstration, ensuring that the prospective customer has sufficient funds to make a purchase, hosting the customer at the vendor's executive briefing center, and conducting a proof-of-concept exercise with members of the customer's staff. Sales management typically reviews the health of their opportunity pipeline on a quarterly basis. They challenge individual account managers as to why specific opportunities have become stuck at a particular stage of development or why other opportunities have been allowed to skip one or more stages.

The pipeline management practices of enterprise IT sales organizations have been honed through years of experience and are actually quite sophisticated. Most IT shops could benefit by adapting such practices to the evaluation of new technology opportunities. Individual IT organizations need to develop their own pipeline framework with explicit gating criteria for transitioning opportunities from one pipeline stage to the next. While there's no universally accepted set of definitions for such criteria, they should address most if not all of the following questions.

- **What are the prospective benefits associated with the use of the new technology under investigation?** Benefits don't need to be explicitly quantified at the earliest stages of evaluation, but benefit targets such as cost reduction, staff productivity, operational risk reduction, etc., should be clearly identified. Benefits should be quantified in progressively greater detail as an opportunity moves through the pipeline to ensure that a formal acquisition business case can be constructed at the end of the process.

- **Do we already possess tools, products, or services that are substantially similar to the new technology?** If so, can we obtain 80 percent of the potential value of the new technology by simply making better use of what we already own? Are the incremental capabilities of the new technology sufficiently valuable to warrant further investigation?

- **Do one or more of our strategic vendors offer comparable capabilities?** If so, should we consider their product as a potential alternative to the technology under evaluation? Additional spending with a strategic vendor may enable us to achieve preferred pricing, deeper discounts, free implementation assistance, or superior support services, not just on the technology under evaluation but on other products as well. Have we fully explored the benefits of considering the alternative offerings of one or more of our strategic vendors?

- **Where will the money come from to purchase the technology if we like it?** Will we be able to fund the purchase through the existing IT budget? Can the purchase be embedded in a business initiative that is currently underway or about to be launched? If not, do we need to seek funds or sponsorship from a business executive outside IT? (If funding from one or more of these sources is unlikely to materialize over the next six to nine months, all further investigation of the product should be suspended. Consider the sales analogy: how much time does a sales representative devote to an opportunity that can't be won within the next three quarters? Sales reps have better uses for their time, and so do the members of the IT team!)

- **Will our company be able to afford this technology on a long-term basis when it's deployed at the scale necessary to achieve enterprise-wide benefits?** The initial investment in a new tool or system might be relatively modest, but is it affordable when deployed more broadly across the enterprise? (For example, a diagnostic tool employed to monitor key aspects of system performance may appear affordable if it is initially applied to a limited number of business-critical systems. But if it were to become essential for the management of all customer-facing systems, would we still likely use this technology or would we revert to a less capable but significantly less costly alternative?)

- **What types of change management issues will we likely encounter if we attempt to implement this new capability?** Will such changes occur primarily within the IT organization or will business users also need to alter their current processes and work practices? Are the leaders of business functions that will be impacted by this technology generally receptive to its adoption? Have change management expenses related to training or incremental support costs been fully incorporated in estimates of the total cost of ownership of this new capability?

- **Which individuals and teams should be involved in substantiating the value of the product?** Perhaps more importantly, when should they become involved? There's a delicate balance between involving potential stakeholders too early or too late in the evaluation process. A mistake in either direction can result in wasted effort, potential rework, or bruised feelings.

As technologists, IT managers tend to focus their attention on the technical capabilities and implementation issues associated with the use of a new technology. But as indicated above, there are a wide range of other questions regarding business benefits, total cost of ownership, operational complexity, vendor management strategies, stakeholder impact, organizational change management, etc., that can easily stop any new technology initiative dead in its tracks. In most instances, these generic issues should take precedence over more narrowly focused technical concerns to avoid wasting time and energy on ideas that will never be implemented.

The generic issues outlined above need to be augmented with "proof points" that are customized for individual opportunities at each pipeline stage. For example, the technical proof points used to shepherd a new storage system or an application testing tool through specific stages of the evaluation process would likely be quite different. The nature of the stakeholders involved in different stages of the process and the scale of their involvement may also differ substantially, depending upon the product under evaluation. Technical integration issues and business scalability concerns may be very product specific and need to be carefully defined for individual stage gates on a product-by-product basis. The gating criteria applied to each opportunity at each stage of the process should represent a mixture of generic and product-specific concerns. No opportunity should receive the attention, time, or resources associated with the next stage of the evaluation process unless it can satisfy the success criteria that have been established for the current stage.

IT organizations need to empanel an appropriate subset of their management team—including several of their most senior managers—in the routine review of their innovation pipeline. The frequency of such reviews depends upon the size of the pipeline and the sense of urgency associated with individual opportunities. The primary responsibility of the oversight team is to avoid the investment of organizational time and energy in proposals of questionable value that might be hard to fund or difficult to implement. As in any innovation endeavor, the goal is to "fail fast" if emerging opportunities cannot meet predetermined success criteria and "fail forward" onto ideas that have the greatest chance of delivering results.

The pipeline assessment process can be readily applied to the stream of new technology ideas being generated by vendors and IT staff members. Internal business partners also need to be co-opted into the process before they fall in love with specific products or services. Experience has shown that once they understand the mechanics of the process and realize that all other technology proposals are being subjected to it, business partners will generally acquiesce and participate. If the process improves the chances of obtaining funding for their proposals, their support typically changes from tacit tolerance to open advocacy!

Historically, the mechanisms IT employed to control the introduction of new technologies within an enterprise were closely coupled to a company's capital investment processes. These mechanisms are increasingly irrelevant in a technology universe dominated by cloud-based services, consumer technologies, and freeware. Legacy capital control mechanisms were primarily focused on the tail end of the evaluation process after considerable energy had been devoted to the validation of new opportunities. In sharp contrast, the pipeline management process outlined above is front-end focused and specifically designed to minimize wasted time and effort.

Innovation labs are organizational DMZs, where technologists and business partners suspend their normal work practices and rules of engagement to evaluate new tools, systems, and hardware. In effect, they are a public admission that innovation is not part of an organization's normal work culture because specialized environments are needed to pursue new ideas. A properly managed pipeline process can make the entire IT organization an innovation lab by soliciting ideas from all team members and involving a broad cross section of relevant stakeholders in the evaluation of new technologies.

Managed Obsolescence

The famous British economist John Maynard Keynes once said, "The difficulty lies not in the new ideas, but in escaping from the old ones." Although he was referring to macroeconomic theories, his words of wisdom are equally applicable to the technology portfolios of modern enterprises. For a wide variety of historical reasons, most companies maintain an eclectic assortment of hardware assets and business applications that represent the sum total of IT decisions made over a period of years or decades. If an IT organization has become proficient in managing a specific technology and employees have become proficient in its use, it can become very difficult to replace or retire.

Although the preceding discussion highlighted the role that IT staff members can play in instigating innovation, their enthusiasm is typically counterbalanced by a strong undertow of staff sentiment that resists change. Many staff members consider the knowledge and experience they've gained with existing technologies to be a form of job security. Consequently, they're not always enthusiastic about the introduction of new capabilities and may actually feel threatened by such initiatives. Others may resist innovation because they fear it will simply result in more work and more operational headaches. If IT management fails to retire aging capabilities while constantly introducing new ones, staff members may exhibit passive-aggressive behaviors in which they seemingly support innovation initiatives while creating a series of roadblocks to the implementation of new capabilities.

Innovation can inadvertently create a two-tier caste system within an IT organization. Individuals involved in evaluating, prototyping, and implementing new technologies typically receive more management attention, access to resources, and career development than staff members who are maintaining legacy systems. It's quite easy for a caste mentality to develop, in which the majority of staff members responsible for the day-to-day operation of existing systems feel that they are second-class citizens. This mentality can create or reinforce the passive-aggressive behaviors referenced above.

Managing obsolescence is a wholly necessary and wholly complementary responsibility of any IT organization that is dedicated to sustained innovation. Many approaches to retiring legacy capabilities have been tried in the past. Larger organizations have attempted to sunset aging capabilities by establishing forward-looking technology standards that bar additional investments in aging technologies. This slow-death approach can actually be counterproductive because it may prolong the existence of specific technologies instead of eliminating them altogether.

Rationalization initiatives have also been employed to reduce the size and complexity of a company's technology holdings. Such initiatives are typically triggered by some external business event such as the acquisition of a company with many duplicative IT capabilities. Rationalization initiatives are also a popular means of reducing IT expenses when the entire enterprise is struggling to survive a downturn in revenues or profitability.

The biggest deterrents to successfully retiring aging technologies are staff complacency and management apathy. Sunsetting and rationalization programs are passing fads within most IT organizations and are associated with specific management regimes. They fail to be institutionalized within the operational fabric of the organization and consequently fail to achieve their long-term goals.

Retiring aging technologies sounds simple in theory but can be extremely complex in practice. Almost by definition, the longer a technology has existed within a company's portfolio the more likely it has been connected to, leveraged by, or integrated with other systems. It's also more likely to be touched by a wide variety of business processes and IT procedures. The devil is in the details as they say, and there are a lot of details that need to be addressed in eliminating existing technologies.

There is no one-size-fits-all program for managing obsolescence. Every IT management team needs to construct a customized program that is sustainable within the company's culture, business model, and organizational structure. Obsolescence programs cannot succeed if they are managed on a part-time basis using Excel spreadsheets. They require dedicated resources, sophisticated project planning, and sustained management support.

Managing obsolescence is simply the other side of the innovation coin. IT leaders are fooling themselves if they believe they can implement a steady stream of new capabilities without reducing the cost, complexity, operational risk, and staff demoralization associated with the maintenance of legacy technologies. Effective leaders will find ways of coupling obsolescence programs with innovation initiatives in ways that make all staff members feel they are involved in and benefiting from the introduction of new capabilities.

That's So GROSS!

The two principal factors that stymie the elimination of older technologies are weak business cases and user resistance. Before the advent of cloud-based services, most corporate technology investments were capitalized and not expensed. Capitalized investments of the past are usually fully depreciated by the time a specific system or infrastructure asset is ripe for retirement. The only tangible savings associated with the elimination of such technologies are recurring maintenance fees, which can be quite modest. Entrenched users who resist the elimination of existing capabilities argue that the savings associated with retirement are small, the business disruption is large, and any potential savings will likely be offset by the cost of replacement capabilities. Users fail to incorporate IT support costs and operational risks in this type of self-serving analysis.

Entrenched users can put up a good fight over the replacement of their tools and systems using these arguments. In many cases, senior business managers are reluctant to overrule the desires of their teams merely to save maintenance expenses, which typically aren't in their budgets anyway! Fighting the retirement battle on a system-by-system or group-by-group basis is tough, and not likely to produce material results.

Material reductions in the number, cost, and complexity of legacy systems can only be achieved through some type of strategic multiyear initiative that is fully endorsed by a company's executive leadership team. In a prior life I launched a program called GROSS, an acronym for Get Rid of Old Stuff Sooner. We scheduled the retirement of a wide variety of aging capabilities on a quarterly basis over a three-year period. While the expense savings associated with the elimination of any single system was relatively small, the total projected savings over the three years was sufficiently large to attract the interest and support of our CFO.

We approached almost every functional group within the company and solicited their participation in GROSS. (We even had buttons made that said "Let's Get GROSS!") End users were generally willing to support the program because of the CFO's highly visible support and with the understanding that any disruption to their business practices would be deferred for several quarters. (I suspect many of them assumed that GROSS was just another management fad that would disappear altogether by the time they were scheduled to retire one or more of their current systems.) GROSS turned out to be a huge success. With the CFO's support and IT's persistence, we eliminated several dozen aging technologies and achieved a net expense reduction of several million dollars.

Chapter 9

Look in the Mirror

Information technology plays an essential role in the daily operation of every large enterprise. Business executives routinely reference their company's IT capabilities as a source of competitive advantage. They sponsor strategic initiatives that leverage IT in new and different ways to grow revenues or expand profits. Even the august *Wall Street Journal* recognized the intrinsic importance of technology by renaming its "Marketplace" news section "Business & Technology" in 2015. In the face of such widespread business agreement about the importance of IT, why are so many IT organizations incapable of launching major technology initiatives that would clearly benefit their companies?

It's easy for IT organizations to become immobilized by the steady stream of requests they receive from their business partners, by the budgetary constraints imposed on their operations, by their own internal skill gaps and bandwidth limitations, and by the transient operational crises that attract undue attention from executive management. Add a dollop of inter-team rivalry within the organization itself and sprinkle liberally with personal animosities among selected staff members, and you have a perfect recipe for organizational paralysis. Trying to plan and implement major, multi-quarter initiatives in this environment is a daunting challenge. Those who have tried and failed rarely try again.

Most IT leaders share a strand of DNA with industry visionaries such as Steve Jobs and Bill Gates that forces them to dream about the transformative impact that IT could potentially have within their companies. However, they're so distracted by customer requests, budgetary constraints, talent deficiencies, operational concerns, and organizational administrivia that they never find the time, energy, or courage to pursue their dreams. The most apt analogy is Gulliver, the fictional English traveler who is immobilized by a race of tiny people after he's washed up on the shores of the mythical kingdom of Lilliput. Gulliver's size and strength far exceed that of any individual Lilliputian, but the Lilliputians are collectively able to tie Gulliver down and render him powerless before he can recover from being shipwrecked. IT organizations have a wealth of knowledge, skills, and experience but they can become similarly immobilized by the steady stream of non-prioritized tasks, demands, requests, and activities they are expected to perform on a regular basis.

Immobilized IT organizations love to play the blame game. They blame their business partners for being overly focused on myopic tactical issues instead of strategic opportunities, for failing to invest time in learning how emerging IT capabilities could deliver future business benefits, or for their inability to collaborate with IT in a constructive fashion. They blame the CFO or COO for failing to provide the discretionary funding required to launch new initiatives. They blame the company for failing to modernize legacy systems, leaving them with a mess of aging and obsolete technology to operate and maintain. They blame new regulatory requirements that siphon off funding and staff to ensure compliance with SOX, HIPAA, PCI, etc. And finally—less openly—individual IT teams blame one another for gaps in technical competence or process discipline that impact the performance of the overall IT organization.

The tone and volume of the blame game are directly modulated by an organization's leaders. If the leaders engage in gratuitous slurs or scornful cynicism about others—be they paying customers, business partners, IT colleagues, or vendors—staff members will take their cues accordingly and amplify the frequency and volume of such remarks. The blame game may provide short-term comic relief for the inmates of an immobilized organization but it does little good in the long term. It only deepens the paralysis of the organization by entrenching the emotional barriers that must be overcome if any type of IT initiative is to succeed in the future.

Living in a Dysfunctional Family

Immobilized IT organizations closely resemble dysfunctional families. According to *Wikipedia*, a *dysfunctional family* is a family in which conflict, misbehavior, and abuse on the part of individual family members occur continually and regularly, leading other members to accommodate such actions. Children who grow up in such families come to believe that such arrangements are normal.

Does this description sound vaguely reminiscent of an IT organization you've worked for in the past, or perhaps the organization currently providing your paycheck? Although it's easier to blame others—especially outsiders—for the ineffectiveness of an IT group, there are many, many ways in which IT groups undermine their own effectiveness. IT leaders can significantly improve the business impact of their teams by simply looking in the mirror and addressing issues that are wholly under their control.

Dysfunctionality within an IT team generally stems from three primary sources. As in any human endeavor, interpersonal issues inevitably develop among team members. Many managers openly ignore or subliminally sanction such issues to avoid conflict. Unresolved interpersonal issues can place significant constraints on the ability of individuals to work together and can introduce unnecessary formality in the way work is performed. Ironically, most IT managers will vehemently argue for a 10 to 20 percent increase in their current staffing levels during every budget cycle but they will do little to resolve interpersonal conflicts among existing staff members that routinely waste 10 to 20 percent of their team's overall time and effort.

The second primary source of dysfunctionality is management's failure to establish clear work priorities. At first glance this statement appears ludicrous. Of course IT managers know that it's their job to assign work to their team members and to prioritize work assignments. In practice, however, IT staff members serve many masters in addition to their direct supervisors. Most staff members receive work requests from project managers leading virtual teams to which they've been assigned, from peers or supervisors on other teams who need their expertise to complete their own work assignments, and from business colleagues outside IT who would like their needs to receive special attention. If managers fail to provide explicit direction or a framework for adjudicating these priorities, team members will prioritize their daily activities based upon their own whims or interests. On one day they may select the hardest task on their personal to-do list because they're seeking a challenge or a learning opportunity. On another day they may choose the easiest, because they have to leave early to attend their daughter's soccer game.

In every IT organization I've ever worked, the staff begs its leaders to provide more clarity about how they should be prioritizing the use of their time. The majority of staff members work on a combination of pressing operational issues, sustaining engineering tasks, business requests, and major projects. Their time is so highly matrixed across multiple tickets, tasks, requests, and projects that they have no idea what constitutes the best use of their time on any given day. Furthermore, they rarely understand how their choices impact the downstream productivity of other team members who are dependent on their work product to get their own jobs done. It's no wonder that business partners frequently exclaim, "IT can't get anything done in less than six months!"

IT Can't Get Anything Done in Less Than Six Months

I once worked for a CEO who became obsessed with the use of Six Sigma techniques to improve the efficiency of our company's internal work processes. He firmly believed that Six Sigma methods could be used to eliminate non-value-added work, limit future increases in labor costs, and improve the satisfaction of our paying customers. The upper ranks of the company's management team were given Six Sigma training, and each business unit was asked to launch at least three Six Sigma projects. This initiative was focused on P&L business units and not on back-office functions such as IT.

In an attempt to support the CEO's Six Sigma program, I personally contacted all the P&L leaders and offered to assign an IT representative to any and all of their initial projects. Much to my surprise, there were no takers. None of the P&L leaders was interested in having IT representation on their teams. When I inquired about the reason, they told me, "When we come out of our Six Sigma workshops we're expected to implement changes to current processes immediately. If our process improvements require changes to IT systems, we wouldn't be able to make any immediate changes, since *everything in IT takes at least six months*" (my emphasis). In effect, IT's participation in the initial projects had been intentionally restricted because the business reengineering teams didn't want to deal with the bureaucracy of the IT organization.

The third primary source of IT dysfunctionality is the series of handoffs that occurs among multiple technical teams, commonly referred to as "IT bureaucracy." In some organizations, individual teams are so overwhelmed by the demands on their time that they establish their own internal work order systems to prioritize tasks. If you want the database analyst team to upgrade the DBMS supporting a specific application, submit a work order. If you need the network engineers to upgrade the circuit capacity of the Cleveland office, submit a work order. If you need the infosec team to enable access to a specific server, submit a work order. Before you know it, all of the teams are employing work orders to complete some of the simplest and frequently recurring workflows within the IT group. This isn't a uniform practice in all organizations, but it commonly exists in larger IT shops and further formalizes the handoff process.

IT bureaucracy drives business partners crazy! Business partners complain that they have to explain their requests and projects over and over again to different members of the IT team. A simple incident or request may be initially reported to an agent on the service desk and then re-reported multiple times as the desk ticket is routed to different technical teams for analysis and resolution. Larger projects require even more repetitive conversations, first with an enterprise architect, who will devise an overall technical solution to a business problem; then with a solution engineer, who will map workflows and dataflows among the components of the solution; then with the project manager, who will deliver the solution; then with a business systems analyst, who will develop test cases for validating the solution; then with the application support group; possibly with the data center team; definitely with the information security team; and so on.

From the business partner's perspective, the project needs to be restarted every time another IT team becomes involved in its execution. The business partner feels that he's become the general contractor for the project, coordinating the activities of multiple IT teams, when he thought that was the responsibility of IT management!

The Tribal Culture of IT Organizations

IT groups portray themselves as full-service organizations composed of small, highly specialized technical teams that work harmoniously to address business needs and challenges. In reality, most operate as tenuous confederations of small, specialized tribes that only come together to defend themselves against common enemies or pursue opportunities of mutual benefit. The nineteenth-century Indian confederations that existed in the western United States provide an apt analogy. They continued to battle one another but could be forced into collective action to protect their territorial claims from common enemies.

Overcoming the tribal boundaries within IT organizations is one of the biggest challenges facing any IT leader. Problems impacting the performance of the organization can't be addressed in any meaningful fashion unless managers are willing to share information about the failings and limitations of individual teams and team members. There are many ways of establishing the trust needed to have such conversations. One of the methods I have explored in the past is to incorporate the family meeting format advocated by family counselors into the initial portion of regularly scheduled staff meetings.

In a family meeting involving smaller children, parents initially solicit compliments from all meeting participants. The parents lavish praise on each child and then go around the table and ask each child to pay a compliment to each of the other participants. Once all of the compliments have been shared, the parents ask each child to identify something he or she doesn't like or wants changed about the way the family is operating. (This entire procedure is something of a ruse, because the parents have convened the meeting specifically to discuss the things they want changed, not necessarily to solicit change proposals from the children!) The obvious intent of the meeting format is to generate self-esteem and goodwill through the sharing of compliments, which can be leveraged to discuss more contentious topics later.

I inserted the compliment portion of the family meeting agenda into my weekly staff meetings at a particular company in the hopes of engendering more open and honest discussion of contentious issues among the members of my management team. We launched the new format without a lot of fanfare. Everyone was receptive and thought it would be fun. Each leader was expected to comment on the positive performance of a staff member or work group outside his personal organization. After the novelty of the new format faded, my direct reports became less and less vocal, frequently passing on the opportunity to pay a compliment to one of their peer organizations. They didn't pass because they lacked respect for the competence or accomplishments of teams outside their direct control, they simply had no knowledge or appreciation of what the other groups actually did. Their personal interactions with individuals outside their immediate span of control was so limited that they had no anecdotal stories to share. Eventually, we abandoned the weekly compliments altogether because the members of the management team were so deeply siloed in the activities of their own teams that they were unable to offer substantive comments on activities being performed elsewhere within the IT organization.

Human nature being what it is, they nevertheless had observations to offer when IT was faced with budget cuts or staffing reductions. When reductions were required, many managers were eager to critique the capabilities or performance of other groups. It seems ironic that they didn't have sufficient knowledge to compliment but had more than enough insight to criticize when they needed to defend their own turfs!

The loss of staff productivity resulting from chronic interpersonal issues, failure to prioritize work activities, and IT bureaucracy can be stunning. The resulting ill will engendered among IT's business partners can be even more damaging. These pervasive issues can only be resolved through management competence and discipline. Solutions do not require fancy new tools or revolutionary processes. IT leaders who are willing to look in the mirror and acknowledge that their organizations exhibit the characteristics of dysfunctional families and are willing to follow the therapeutic suggestions outlined below will end up with happier employees, more productive teams, and more appreciative business partners.

The Fifth Amendment

Readers who believe that their organizations are top-quartile performers in terms of efficiency and effectiveness can test that perception with the following mental experiment. Suppose you had a rich uncle who recently bequeathed his privately owned manufacturing company to you. Before he passed away, your uncle employed consultants to construct an IT strategy that would enable his company to expand global operations and double in size over the next three years. The consultants recommended the implementation of a single material requirements planning (MRP) system to support all manufacturing activities, a complete overhaul of the company's retail website, and a total upgrade of the company's network backbone. Assuming you agreed with these recommendations and were prepared to fund them, would you be willing to employ your current IT organization to perform the necessary work or would you seek alternative implementation contractors? Hint: if you don't believe that your current organization would be able to perform the work as effectively or efficiently as other potential contractors, this is the point at which you invoke the Fifth Amendment!

Stop Administering People and Start Managing Them

As an IT manager, it's quite possible to administer annual performance reviews, conduct career planning discussions, and establish engagement survey action plans without providing honest performance feedback to your team or its members. Some IT teams have terrible reputations for being incompetent or unresponsive, but their members come to work every day convinced they are doing a terrific job managing their assigned responsibilities. Similarly, individuals will sit through their annual performance reviews and focus exclusively on the five compliments they receive instead of the two suggestions for improvement. (IT managers frequently contribute to their employees' selective hearing by spending the first forty-five minutes of such reviews lavishing praise and then hurriedly pointing out one or two areas for improvement during the last ten minutes of the conversation.)

As discussed elsewhere in this book, no manager—no matter how smart he is, or how well organized he is, or how little sleep he needs—can perform all the tasks assigned to his team. Every manager ultimately realizes that his personal success depends upon his ability to work effectively through his team members. In turn, the effectiveness of his team members is directly dependent upon the feedback they receive regarding their performance and developmental needs, both individually and collectively. The manager who fails to provide such feedback is compromising the effectiveness of his team, unwittingly forcing himself to assume more direct control of routine activities and inevitably undermining his own success.

Sadly, the annual performance review process employed in most companies is probably the least effective means of providing individuals with performance feedback. That sounds like a contradictory statement, but it's true. Most employees receive very little performance feedback on a regular basis. I'm not referring to gratuitous "attaboy" comments or suggestions about how to build a better PowerPoint slide in the future. Substantive feedback is based upon serious insightful comments regarding the manner in which work activities were organized, prioritized, and implemented; the skill sets or behaviors that an individual needs to expand or develop; and the manner in which an individual collaborates with others. In the absence of incremental feedback, many employees approach their annual performance review with fear and trepidation. They treat it as a summary judgment of their net worth to the corporation. It's unreasonable to expect anyone to take nuanced improvement suggestions to heart if they consider their annual review discussion to be a definitive appraisal of their short-term job security!

The common failure to provide incremental performance feedback to IT team members is doubly sad because the perpetual stream of tasks, activities, and projects that occur throughout the organization present a wealth of feedback opportunities. Individuals are much more able to assimilate bite-sized feedback regarding an activity or project than summary feedback administered through the annual review process. Enlightened leaders present new assignments to their team members as developmental opportunities and place particular emphasis upon the skills or capabilities the individual should strive to develop over the course of the assignment. Highlighting developmental opportunities at the outset of a new assignment logically sets the stage for a feedback conversation at its conclusion. Managers could avoid the drama and emotions that accompany many annual performance reviews by simply having short, project-specific or activity-specific feedback conversations over the course of the year. This type of incremental feedback is typically easier to deliver, easier to assimilate, and more readily accepted than summary feedback delivered on an annual basis.

Managers who persistently sidestep their performance management responsibilities do a profound disservice to their team members and ultimately to themselves. Successful leaders are invariably successful people managers. If aspiring leaders consistently find their people management responsibilities to be tiresome or uncomfortable, they should pursue alternative roles as individual contributors or technical leaders, because their inability to accomplish work through the activities of others will eventually be self-limiting.

Start Prioritizing and Simplifying

IT organizations are capable of producing impressive results when their priorities are clearly defined by business executives. If a new territory assignment system needs to be functional ten weeks before the annual sales kickoff meeting, it will be delivered on time. If five thousand employees within a newly acquired company need to have fully functional SAP accounts on the first day of merged operations, the five thousand accounts will be established on time. If a new HR benefits service needs to be available to all company employees on the first day of the annual open enrollment period, that will happen too. IT organizations may struggle to establish and enforce internal priorities, but when priorities are deemed to be business critical by its external clients, most organizations will deliver on their commitments. The political consequences of failure are too dire, and the entire organization will rally around the need to keep its business partners happy.

Unfortunately, organizational clarity about IT's work priorities rarely occurs. Even when such priorities exist, they are typically stated in broad terms that aren't all that useful in determining the tasks that individual staff members need to complete today, tomorrow, or by Friday. In most cases, managers and staff members are juggling a broad assortment of incidents, requests, and assigned tasks that resist easy prioritization. As business demands increase and IT staffing levels stay constant (or decrease), work prioritization becomes a critical management competency within every IT shop. New tools and processes are needed to ensure that team members are not just doing a lot of things, but are doing the *right* things at the right time.

Scrum procedures employed by software development teams can be applied more broadly to any set of interrelated work tasks, especially in situations where team members have serial dependencies on one another to complete a particular work assignment. Scrums are typically short, stand-up team meetings in which team members report their individual progress since their last meeting, discuss and agree upon their immediate work plans, and commit to completing certain actions or deliverables before the next meeting. Some individuals might claim that scrums are a waste of time, just another meeting that reduces the time they have available for real work. Properly facilitated, scrums serve exactly the opposite purpose. They ensure that each individual is making the best use of her time, not just to optimize her personal productivity but the productivity of the entire team. Experience has shown that scrum members typically do a better job of fulfilling the expectations they establish with one another than in meeting deadlines established by their managers. Most managers have such a limited understanding of the demands on their employees' time that they may actually be the least qualified individuals to predict when certain objectives or deliverables can actually be achieved.

Kanban systems are another popular means of prioritizing tasks for individual team members. Kanban systems employ color-coded cards stacked in a sequential order to reflect the relative priority of the individual tasks recorded on each card. Managers review and reorder the card sequence on a regular basis, sometimes daily or weekly. Team members "pull" a new card after completing a task and are, by definition, working on the next most important activity within their work queue. Kanban systems should ideally merge work requirements emanating from production support, work order, and project management systems. But even in the absence of perfect integration, they can still help individual team members manage their time more effectively.

Finally, there are a wide variety of cloud-based collaboration tools that team members can use to ask questions, report progress, and share information with one another. These tools merge various types of chat, videoconferencing, file sharing, document management, calendaring, project management, and email capabilities to improve internal team communications. They are particularly useful for virtual teams whose members reside in multiple geographic locations.

The primary goal of all of these frameworks and tools is to ensure that individual staff members are prioritizing their time in ways that address the most significant needs of their clients and colleagues, while also optimizing the overall productivity of their teams.

Few IT teams receive accolades for the breadth of activities they perform. Almost invariably, IT groups receive recognition for performing certain essential services extremely well or for completing strategic projects on time and on budget. Successful IT leaders resist the temptation to find more things for their organization to do. Instead, they focus the strengths and energies of their team on recurring activities and special projects that have the greatest business significance. As the Chinese philosopher Lao Tzu once said: "To attain knowledge add things every day. To attain wisdom subtract things every day." Wise IT leaders routinely follow Lao Tzu's advice.

Before There Were Scrums

The idea of bringing coworkers together to discuss near-term work plans is not as revolutionary as some scrum masters would lead you to believe. I visited a start-up company more than fifteen years ago that was developing a new data storage appliance. The company consisted of roughly twenty-five individuals and had received $4 million in venture capital funding. They were singularly focused on constructing a working prototype of the proposed appliance. A large-format engineering diagram of the appliance was hung in the group's breakout area. All of the company's employees assembled in the breakout area every morning, where they were joined by the company founder. The founder would point at the schematic diagram hanging on the wall and announce, "If you spend any time today working on anything other than that (i.e., the appliance), you are wasting time!" This ritual was repeated on a daily basis. They didn't call this meeting a scrum, but with twenty-twenty hindsight, it sure felt like one to me.

I had personal experience with scrum-like meetings when I served as the Program Scientist for a Space Shuttle radar mission. NASA had funded a team of forty scientists from around the world to collect radar imagery for a wide variety of botanical, geological, agricultural, and environmental studies. Mission planning was complicated by a variety of factors including the attitude of the Shuttle, the work schedule of the astronauts, and the capacity of the Shuttle's onboard data storage system. The final data collection plan was constructed over a four-week period. The planning team met twice daily during this period, at the beginning and end of each day, to discuss trade-offs between the competing scientific requests, the Shuttle's operational constraints, and data storage/transmission capabilities on an orbit-by-orbit basis. In effect, we held two scrum meetings per day to ensure we were working on the most critical issues that needed to be resolved to construct a viable data-collection plan. It sounds exhausting but it was actually incredibly stimulating and very successful.

The lesson to be learned from both experiences is that work groups can be extraordinarily productive if they communicate with one another and review their priorities on a regular basis. As obvious as this sounds, most IT knowledge workers spend their days in semi-isolation, staring at PC monitors instead of discussing issues, sharing information, or making personal commitments to other team members.

Manufacture Time and Minimize Handoffs

The number of repetitive tasks and recurring workflows within IT organizations is mind numbing. Fortunately, a wide variety of automation tools are available to reduce the manual labor required to perform such activities. Unfortunately, far too few organizations establish dedicated automation teams or provide the necessary training to realize the full benefits of such tools. In some instances, selected team members may actually resist automation initiatives because they believe their manual roles in established work processes provide them with personal job security. Team members frequently argue that workflow automation exposes the organization to too many unknown operational risks, when in fact they are simply trying to protect their jobs.

Experience has shown that you can't simply train everyone on a specific tool and then turn them all loose to apply the tool to their individual work activities. There typically needs to be some governance regarding when, where, and how a tool is to be used and some consistency in its actual application. Automation centers of excellence—whether dedicated or virtual—can pay big dividends in avoiding duplication of effort and leveraging opportunities for reusing automation scripts and playbooks.

Automation campaigns can produce a wide variety of benefits. They can increase the bandwidth of individual teams, freeing up team members to work on higher-priority or higher-value tasks. They can reduce the friction and delay times created by serial handoffs of interrelated tasks when applied to work processes that span multiple technical teams. By definition, they reduce the risk of human error. Finally, they can materially improve the satisfaction of IT customers by accelerating mundane tasks such as password resets, server provisioning, laptop reimaging, new employee onboarding, etc. (They can even improve the job satisfaction of initial naysayers when such individuals receive more interesting or more challenging work assignments after some of their repetitive tasks have been automated away!)

Successful automation campaigns feed on themselves and produce recurring benefits. Groups deploying new tools for the first time or applying existing tools to a new group of processes are typically quite cautious and retain a significant number of manual touchpoints in the automated process. As familiarity with the tool grows and experience with its application expands, groups invariably eliminate more and more of the manual intervention points in the automated process. Database provisioning times that formerly took weeks may initially take days. Code release windows that formerly were performed over two work shifts may initially be performed over one shift. As familiarity and confidence grows, these types of processes and others can be routinely performed in hours or minutes, in many instances through end-user self-service.

Automation can pay major productivity dividends if it is pursued in an organized fashion. Piecemeal adoption of different tools and automation frameworks by disparate teams will yield marginal benefits at best.

Epilogue

The Art of the Possible

Every true IT leader hopes to transform his group into a high-performance team that can accelerate the growth and boost the profitability of his company. A team's effectiveness can be transformed by reengineering work practices, adopting new tools, developing new skills, and automating repetitive processes. A team's impact can be transformed by devising initiatives that expose the company to new markets, new customers, or new products, or that enhance the retention and value of existing customers. Business impact can also be achieved by leveraging technology in ways that improve the efficiency and agility of a company's internal operations.

Every true leader has these aspirations, but few are able to truly transform the internal performance or external impact of their teams. Successful leaders have to be visionary, enthusiastic, and persistent agents of change. They need to battle a vast array of forces that actively resist and passively subvert changes to the status quo.

When you stop to think about all the obstacles that impede change within a large enterprise, it's quite remarkable that any substantive changes occur at all. Adverse business conditions, the rise of competitors, merger or acquisition initiatives, executive turnover, and business line reorganizations invariably limit the resources and management attention that can be devoted to transformational IT change. Cultural prejudices regarding the role, capabilities, or effectiveness of the IT organization may further limit management's receptivity to change. IT team members themselves may explicitly or implicitly resist change due to their personal skill limitations, job security concerns, local work cultures, or time to retirement.

IT change initiatives are also thwarted by constant changes in business expectations and the inescapable demands of everyday operations. Perennial demands for IT cost cutting can be replaced overnight with demands for innovation when a competitor suddenly introduces a new technology-enabled product or service. Chronic complaints about IT crippling the productivity of the workforce by locking down PC images, blocking access to external websites, and restricting access to company data can be replaced overnight by demands for more stringent security safeguards following a major breach or intrusion. IT initiatives that are considered to be critical or essential in one environment may suddenly be perceived to be out of step with current business needs when management expectations change.

Even in organizations where IT team members embrace change and business leaders are receptive to technology initiatives, change agendas can languish indefinitely simply because everyone is preoccupied with the demands of everyday business. IT leaders who evangelize transformational changes within their organizations will inevitably hear one or more of their team members plaintively exclaim, "I already have a full-time job. I can't do that job and launch off on this new initiative unless you identify someone who can take over my current responsibilities!"

Otto von Bismarck, the proverbial Iron Chancellor who unified the German states in the nineteenth century, was one of the earliest and arguably most famous practitioners of realpolitik. Realpolitik refers to the pragmatic conduct of politics or diplomacy without regard for ideological notions or moral concerns. Practitioners of realpolitik seek success within the world of today, not within the world of their dreams or imagination. They acknowledge the practical constraints and implicit boundary conditions that restrict their options and seek the greatest benefits that can be achieved under current circumstances.

Bismarck referred to politics as "the art of the possible." At the risk of offending any political scientists who may be reading this book, I believe that effective IT leadership can also be defined as the art of the possible. As described above, the forces that resist change within an enterprise are extensive and dynamic. Successful IT leaders need the experience and intuition to detect those rare moments when forces are aligned in such a manner that substantive change can actually be implemented. However, intuition is not enough. True leaders also need the courage to seize such opportunities before they evaporate. And above all they need the political capital required to enlist the active support or passive acquiescence of all relevant stakeholders in their cause.

Organizational alignments that are conducive to substantive change occur with the frequency of a solar eclipse or the passing of an interplanetary comet. They occur when there's a clear business need, a positive track record of IT accomplishment, trust between IT and business leaders, access to investment dollars, and enthusiasm within the IT team to go somewhere they've never gone before. Similarly, internal IT transformations occur when team members embrace the need for change and are willing to undertake the reskilling, process reengineering, technology changes, and organizational restructuring that such transformations entail.

Too many IT leaders are plagued by romantic notions about how to promote and facilitate meaningful change. Some resemble Don Quixote. They operate as self-styled evangelists of innovation who wander ceaselessly throughout their companies espousing transformative initiatives that rarely, if ever, gain traction. Others suffer from a subliminal love of heroism. They hope to obtain accolades for themselves and their teams by implementing cutting-edge IT capabilities that deliver undeniable business benefits. Although bumbling suitors frequently emerge as heroes during the last ten minutes of many romantic movies, similar heroic successes rarely happen in the real-life world of enterprise IT.

What IT really needs is more Iron Chancellors, individuals who possess uncanny insight into the art of the possible and exploit every substantive change opportunity to advance their strategic goals and objectives.

Transformative change seldom occurs through one-time management proclamations or decisive political battles. Successful transformations are implemented over a period of years, not months or quarters. They occur through a series of small unit actions—meetings, decisions, and achievements—that convert skeptics and end up transforming the transformation itself into an integral part of everyday business. As paradoxical as it sounds, transformations are complete when they are no longer considered to be transformations by their participating stakeholders!

Transformational success has conventionally been framed in terms of what IT can do for the business. That needs to change. Future transformational success will be measured in terms of what IT can do *with* the business.

IT's role in the enterprise has changed substantially over the past ten years. SaaS applications have been adopted on a wholesale basis to support a wide variety of business-critical processes. Consumer technologies have proliferated within many companies—largely over the objections of IT organizations—because such technologies help employees perform their everyday duties more efficiently. Development teams are leveraging the infrastructure services of public cloud providers and assuming broader responsibilities for supporting production systems as DevOps concepts are incorporated into everyday work practices.

On one hand, these changes should be celebrated as clear examples of the assimilation of IT capabilities into the day-to-day functioning of the enterprise. On the other hand, they also represent the disintermediation of IT organizations from many of their conventional roles and responsibilities.

IT teams engage in endless discussions about enabling business processes, delivering services to their business partners, improving service quality, ensuring customer satisfaction, and aligning their activities with business needs. In spite of this incessant internal chatter about customer service and business alignment, most employees in large enterprises—both managers and staff members—consider IT to be an obstacle that must be ignored or overcome in order to get real work done. The disconnect between IT's internal service provider mentality and employee perceptions regarding IT's utility is actually quite large in most companies. Unfortunately, it's rarely discussed in a meaningful way because employees and business managers have largely resigned themselves to the current state of affairs.

Successful IT leaders of the future will find ways of integrating their teams into the business cultures of their companies and overcoming the us-versus-them mentality that is so pervasive today. They will shun the limelight and seek recognition as the business's Teammate of the Year instead of trying to become its Most Valuable Player. They will constantly be on the lookout for those rare opportunities where obstacles to change can be overcome through intuition, courage, and hard work. They will earn the right to assist in the transformation of their companies by first transforming themselves and their teams.

Abbreviations Glossary

24×7 24 hours per day multiplied by 7 days per week
B2C business to consumer
BSA business systems analyst
CEO chief executive officer
CFO chief financial officer
CIO chief information officer
CMDB configuration management database
CRM customer relationship management
CTO chief technology officer
DBMS database management system
DevOps development and operations
DMZ demilitarized zone
ERP enterprise resource planning
G&A general and administrative expenses
HIPAA Health Insurance Portability and Accountability Act regulations
HiPo high potential
IaaS infrastructure as a service
ITIL information technology infrastructure library
NFL National Football League
NPS National Park Service

OCD obsessive-compulsive disorder
OMB Office of Management and Budget
PaaS platform as a service
PC personal computer
PCI Payment Card Industry regulations
P&L profit and loss
PMI Project Management Institute
POC proof of concept
QBR quarterly business review
QSR quarterly service review
R&D research and development
SaaS software as a service
SCM supply chain management
SEC Securities and Exchange Commission
SOA service-oriented architecture
SOX Sarbanes-Oxley financial regulations
VP vice president
Y2K year 2000 transition

Acknowledgments

The idea of writing a book on IT management crept onto my professional bucket list several years ago. After leading IT organizations at several companies and establishing relationships with many of my peers, I gradually came to realize that the issues, failures, and frustrations I had personally experienced as a CIO were chronic in nature and widely shared across the IT industry. On a particularly bad day it seemed as if all IT professionals in leadership positions were making the same mistakes and suffering from the same problems over and over again. This book is my humble attempt to break that cycle by sharing observations and providing advice that will enable the next generation of IT leaders to avoid the management sins of the past!

This book is a direct outcome of the relationships and experiences I have shared with the IT leaders and business executives I have worked with in the past. I owe them a debt of gratitude. They have certainly taught me more than I ever taught them.

I also wish to thank all of my professional peers and acquaintances. Many have invited me into their organizations and have been extremely open in sharing their problems, as well as their successes. I have been fortunate to develop an extensive network of professional peers and have benefited enormously from their perspectives and advice.

First-time authors need a lot of encouragement to get their books across the finish line. I want to especially thank Martha Heller, Hunter Muller, Karen Garcia, Rodney Fullmer, Rusty Perry, and Allen Touchet for their ongoing encouragement and support.

The original manuscript benefited significantly from thoughtful reviews provided by Von Rhea at Trimble, Simon King at Numerify, Chris Flynn at PriceWaterhouse Coopers, Scott Lemberger at DigitalGlobe, and Gwen Curlee. I sincerely appreciate their insightful feedback.

Finally, I'd like to thank Erika Heilman, Jill Friedlander, Jill Schoenhaut, Susan Lauzau, Ari Choquette, and the team at Bibliomotion. Publishing a book for the first time is a little like an Eskimo buying a house for the first time: you don't always know what questions you should be asking! The Bibliomotion team has patiently guided me to the right questions, kept me on schedule, and made the overall publishing experience as painless as it could possibly be.

It obviously takes a team to publish a book. I am genuinely grateful to everyone referenced above but take full responsibility for the observations and advice presented in this publication.

Index

Index

About the Author

Mark Settle dreamt of being an astronaut during the earliest stages of his career. He obtained advanced degrees in geology and spent four years as an Air Force officer before becoming a Program Scientist at NASA Headquarters Following this extensive flirtation with the public sector, he joined the oil and gas industry, where he received his first practical introduction to IT management within a large commercial enterprise. Over the past two decades he has served as the Chief Information Officer of six public companies and has broad business experience in the information services, enterprise software, consumer products, high-tech distribution, financial services, and oil and gas industries. Mark Settle has received multiple awards and is a three-time CIO 100 honoree. He serves on the advisory boards of several venture capital firms and advises a variety of start-up companies. This book summarizes the practical lessons he has learned through a long, distinguished, and wholly unanticipated career in IT management.